THE HUNGRY SELF

Books by Kim Chernin

CROSSING THE BORDER

THE FLAME BEARERS (*a novel*)

THE HUNGRY SELF

THE HUNGER SONG (*poetry*)

IN MY MOTHER'S HOUSE

THE OBSESSION

REINVENTING EVE

SEX AND OTHER SACRED GAMES
  (*with Renate Stendahl*)

THE
HUNGRY SELF

Women, Eating, and Identity

KIM CHERNIN

HarperPerennial

A Division of HarperCollins*Publishers*

First Perennial Library edition published 1986. First HarperPerennial edition published 1994.

Library of Congress Cataloging-in-Publication Data

Chernin, Kim.
    The hungry self : women, eating, and identity / Kim Chernin.
       p.   cm.
    ISBN 0-06-092504-3 (pbk.)
    1. Eating disorders. 2. Women—Mental health. 3. Identity (Psychology).
    4. Mothers and daughters. I. Title.
    RC552.E18C48   1994
    616.85´26´0082—dc20   93-41851

94 95 96 97 98 CW 10 9 8 7 6 5 4 3 2

For Michael

Contents

Foreword to the HarperPerennial Edition

WHEN I FIRST BEGAN to write seriously, in my early twenties, I used to think writing was for lofty topics, not for humble intimacies about food. I had always planned to write (someday) a visionary book about the transformation of women, a grand scheme complete with steps and stages, calls and awakenings. It used to puzzle me that my obsession with food became my first public statement. Then, having written one book about this uncomfortable topic (*The Obsession*, 1981), it puzzled me even more when I found myself writing another.

I started *The Hungry Self* in 1984. By then, I had begun to work as a consultant to women with eating disorders. This too was puzzling, for I had not yet gone back to graduate school for a degree in psychology. I was a woman who had suffered and thought, written and spoken. When other women called, when they wanted to come talk with me, I was at pains to clarify who I was (only a writer) and was not (not yet a therapist). It always made me smile secretly when professional or academic reviewers of my books on some occasions seemed to think I should have written more scholarly, more researched works, when my intention had been all along to write about a woman suffering and thinking about her experience. I knew there was a place for books by unaffiliated, reflective women speaking to others like themselves. Because I hadn't planned to make myself an expert, I was genuinely surprised when the success of *The Obsession* allowed me to have weighty opinions about other women's lives. If indeed I deserved to hold these opinions, it was not because of my academic and professional qualifications, and that was the point. I had come to my opinions by virtue of studying my own life. Therefore, what I was capable of accomplishing others could accomplish too. That is how I reasoned. Others, meaning other women, people like myself who had not (necessarily) gained their self-knowledge through an advanced degree. It was for them my book had been written.

By the time I came to write *The Hungry Self*, however, I was no longer, even in my own eyes, an upstart analyst of our culture's troubled relation to women. By then I had spoken in depth for many hours to other women, had begun to learn from them as they came, session by session, to explore with me the deep underground of a distress so intimate it had frequently not been confided to therapists and analysts, even after years of therapeutic work. As the women with whom I was working went deeper into their dilemma, I too began to move into a deeper understanding of my own, so that in time the entire question of women and food began to show itself to me in a new light and I began to think of an eating disorder as holding the key to unfathomed mysteries of female existence.

This view finally made sense out of the stubborn tenacity of eating disorders and obsessions: the way they can suddenly disappear one day, giving an illusion of resolution, only to pop up again a few months later, or at the next crucial turning point in a woman's life. The women with whom I was working seemed always to need yet greater understanding, to go further in an exploration of symptoms and sufferings, as if there were a story trying to emerge, which had almost been grasped, yet was still somehow eluding us, so more tough work was required as we were being pushed beyond what we knew.

The Hungry Self was written out of this hunger for meaning. When it was published in 1985, no one was surprised at the media interest in the book. The news stories about the numbers of women of all ages who suffered from anorexia and bulimia were now common. I was prepared to go on the road once again with my message. But this time, I was taken by surprise by the absence in the radio and television media of that feminist sisterhood that had welcomed *The Obsession*. None of the women I had spoken to only a few years earlier were still at their jobs. Frequently, I was interviewed by men who seemed to have no idea why my ideas were being taken seriously, if they were being taken seriously, which they seemed to doubt. I felt a hostility I had not felt before, a dismissive lack of credible interest. Most interviewers had not bothered to read my book, and among those who had read it, there was a kind of stubborn refusal, I thought, to consider the deep issues it raised.

Often, I had the impression media people were less prepared than several years before to take the suffering of an eating disorder seriously. Just beneath the surface of many conversations, I heard, or seemed to hear, the scornful insistence, "Come on, you can't be serious. Women going on a diet are feeling guilt about their mothers?"

It isn't easy to talk about serious ideas in the television format, where one is expected to show up, say a few glib words, and move on to the next show. This is especially difficult when you have been given the opportunity to reach millions of women who might not otherwise come across the ideas you've been mulling over with yourself. I was reluctant to produce formulaic replies (we did not yet speak of sound bites). I wanted my message to arise spontaneously from the moment in which it was asked, so that the spontaneity might carry it straight into the heart of a woman in distress. I wanted to reach people.

I was flying all over the country, doing the talk show circuit, speaking in bookstores, arriving for hurried conversations at radio stations, fretting about the fact that over the years there seemed to be a diminishing popular understanding of eating disorders, while at the same time an entire field of professional inquiry, research, publication, and treatment had grown up.

In retrospect, it is evident that this retreat from understanding was already a backlash, a retreat from meaning, a refusal to understand. Even the point I had made several years earlier, that an eating disorder could be seen as a reflection of a culture's troubled relationship to its women, seemed to have lost ground. With *The Hungry Self,* I argued that this trouble could have penetrated so deeply into the female psyche that it had caused women to experience what amounted to a generational breakdown.

While on the road, I began to get the impression I had been invited to most interviews because someone imagined I was going to speak about diets. Several times I was paired with women from weight-loss organizations, who themselves seemed puzzled by my tendency to bring up philosophical and analytic questions about female hunger. Often, during the commercial break, members of the show's staff rushed up to whisper that I should leave out the philosophy, get down to business. At times, I had to stop the host from overtly dismissing what I had to say, as he turned back to the concrete questions of losing weight.

This tension, between the interviewers and me, did not keep a considerable rapport from growing between me and the members of the audience, most of whom were women. That was when I experienced directly, for myself, how thoroughly most forms of mass media, including book publishing, underestimate the intelligence of women, our need to understand in depth, with subtlety and complexity, our troubled relationship to our culture.

I had made this argument from the time I had first attempted to publish *The Obsession*, when I was told by several publishers that it was "too intelligent for women." I had made it again in an attempt to persuade my publishers to get enough books into the stores to meet what I suspected would be the demand for them. I had to make it again now in every television studio across the country. Left to themselves, the women in the audience had no trouble with my "philosophizing." During station breaks the conversation between us would continue, growing more serious and urgent than the talk show host could allow. The countdown would begin, the inevitable signal that the show was going back on the air, the host would get the topic back to the appropriate level of triviality, I would refuse to engage in it at that level, the tension would become perceptible and finally, about midway through my tour, I lost patience. While we were on the air I told the host he had not read my book, didn't seem to grasp what I was talking about, and that in his comments about women and weight he had insulted the women in the audience. Unruffled by my challenge, he turned with a cavalier gesture to the audience. Did they feel insulted? Their response clearly took him by surprise. "Yes," the women cried out. "Yes," they felt insulted, indeed he was not listening to me; they had come to hear me speak about mothers and daughters and women's struggle for identity, and he was not letting me get to the point.

It is dangerous to underestimate the intelligence of women. Large numbers of women we consider uneducated, not well read, whom we think of as simple people, homemakers or merely mothers, reveal an inherent capacity for analytical and cultural understanding when it comes to the suffering of their daughters or nieces, or their own often silenced conflicts. I myself have had to learn this all over again so many times during initial telephone conversations, in first sessions, during ongoing analytic work, when women are invited to piece together the meaning of their sufferings.

More than ever, therefore, I had no desire to present myself as an "expert." I did not wish to take advantage of my status as a published writer of (by then) four books. I wanted everyone to understand that the way I had come to think about myself, with complexity, cultural breadth, psychological nuance, was also possible for most any woman who sat down to think. I refused the implications that my authority was conferred from outside, that I was presumed to know, to have a right to speak, for any reason other than that I had found a voice.

In bringing my book out into the world, I was a new kind of crusader, tougher, bolder in my self-assertion. I knew by now that I did not speak only for myself, or the handful of women I had interviewed for my first book. As the tour went on, my conviction grew that our media culture would not take readily to the type of analysis I had to offer about daughters who felt like survivors, about mothers whose lives had been unfulfilled, about the hidden drama of envy and resentment between mothers and daughters of our time. I found it exhausting and finally pointless to urge this message against the talk show enthusiasm for the easily digested.

I decided to cut short my tour. I turned down the invitation to any number of high-publicity national shows. I had decided that if my book spoke to the women of my time I could leave the book to make its own way. I went home, back to work with the women who had reached out to me because they had read my work. In the privacy of my consultation room, there was no talk show host to trivialize the female suffering about food and the female body.

Nevertheless, the tendency to dismiss female suffering enters the consultation room. It comes up in me every time I sit down to write about eating disorders. Each time, I have to overcome a strange, persistent prejudice against them as a serious topic. One knows and simultaneously refuses to know; one grasps and imme- diately loses one's grip on truth. This happens frequently as my conversations with women about female hunger become more elaborate over time, branching out to cover every conceivable aspect of a woman's life from the first moments of life, earliest childhood, through all the tangled twistings of bonds and attachments, down through the generations. If this seems overstated, I cannot apologize. I believe it to be true, although I myself can repeatedly lose touch with that truth and have to struggle back to the authentic issues.

The female body has a story to tell. In its hunger, its hidden shame, its shadowy sense of guilt, there is the still as yet not fully articulated indictment of our culture's treatment of women. We do not yet know just how many women break down when their periods begin, when they can no longer hope against hope, or believe against reality that after all they will not become women. With that first blood comes the certainty, as they imagine it, that they will be consigned to lives as restricted, as impoverished as those of their mothers. Young girls coming of age pull out their pubic hair, they pound their thighs with fists, they go on diets, they attempt to starve themselves, they purge with laxatives, they vomit several times a day. Of course, it begins to sound sensational; there is scarcely a way, as yet, to speak convincingly of this hidden grief in spite of the numerous books now written about eating disorders. There is scarcely a way, as yet, to convince ourselves, to know beyond doubt, to make part of ourselves the degree, the depth, the intensity of distress at being a woman. Back behind an eating disorder there may be a story of childhood sexual abuse, a tale of neglect in a family whose abundance and prosperity are intended only for its boys. One may discover a father uneasy about a daughter's maturing body, a mother who cannot easily send her daughters off into a world larger than the world she knew.

It is no wonder we all tend to share a reluctance to look too deeply into matters that seem easier to keep superficial. Most of us would prefer to think of our suffering with the female body as vanity, to hide generational problems by the counting of calories, to express in the code of inches and pounds the severe, persisting doubt, even after decades of feminist thought, about the role of women in our culture.

To many women an eating disorder may at times seem to be a Pandora's box. Once opened, the hidden troubles of a life pour out. We awaken from our innocence (ours was a happy family), turn back to look again at how we grew up (mother was unhappy), turn over again the stories we have repeated to ourselves so many times (I was to blame for their unhappiness. It wasn't the trouble in my parents' marriage). I am no longer surprised that most of us, although we have the capacity to understand ourselves deeply, simultaneously are willing to swallow the easy answers dished out to us as we thumb through the latest issue of almost any magazine for its most recent diet.

Our resistance to understanding cannot be blamed on us, although we are the only ones who can break through it. There is something forbidden about a serious understanding of ourselves as women. We leap back from it as if we had just touched a hot stove, for it is without doubt a species of cultural undercover work, and therefore not for the fainthearted.

But after all, an eating disorder is not a Pandora's box. Without doubt, it will run us a good chase before we are done; we will have had to set loose on it our keenest understanding. Only then will it be able to deliver its transformative potential. I know how abundant the outcome can be, if only we are able to resist the easy answers. Urgency, anxiety, a profound sense of insecurity, a lack of an appropriate (large enough) identity, all seek a quick fix. We ask, "But what can I do about this hunger and obsession?" as if we have not yet realized that understanding *is* doing, perhaps the most, maybe the only effective kind.

When the temptation for the quick fix sets on me I go back to my bookshelves. I make myself read even my own work over again, although I have never known a writer happy with anything she has written much more than a year ago. I also read whatever else I can find about eating disorders, particularly those first-person accounts of women who have suffered and seen themselves through. Theories are fine, and I will advance quite a few myself in this book; but in the end, no theory can reach the power of a woman telling her own story, or the story of other women as it was told to her.

And then of course there are the popular magazines. Recently, a client of many years, who has just stopped being bulimic, brought into my consultation room some half-dozen photographs. One series accompanied a story about a woman recovering from anorexia who had decided to have herself photographed during her most severe period of emaciation. The other series was from an article about young models, who were regarded as the "face of beauty to come." My client was appalled by these fashion photographs, raised her voice, shook the pages torn from recent magazines, and asked me with considerable urgency, "Why don't the mothers do anything about this? Don't they know what this will do to their daughters?"

I understood her distress. After several years of gradually changing imagery of women, who over the last decade had begun to appear strapping and athletic, occasionally almost buxom, even in fashion magazines, there has recently been a sudden reversal, an iconoclastic backlash, a retreat into the gaunt, emaciated, drooping, wilted, baby-doll femininity many women thought had gone forever.

It was not only this unwelcome return that distressed my client, or the fact that these young beauties, "sans artifice," and " without attitude," as the article claimed, had a disturbing physical kinship with the anorexic. There was something more sinister in these photographs, which became apparent to me too when, studying them at my desk over many days, I noticed an uncanny similarity in the facial expressions of the model in the floral chiffon dress and the naked anorexic woman gazing out at the camera.

These faces were haunted. The model's face no less than the anorexic's, perhaps the model's expression even more disturbing, although both women shared the same long face, high cheekbones, limp hair, set mouths, troubled eyes. For all her anguish, the anorexic woman looked angry, as if she was still planning to fight back. The model looked defeated, broken, as if she had withdrawn solidly into the hopelessness of her condition, which she only barely managed to disguise with her Safari Climate Response Lip SPF in Blush by Ralph Lauren.

The ambiguities of an eating disorder implicate several thousand years of culture, as I once said grandiloquently at the end of a brief radio show. I guess books are the place to make such assertions after all. Readers at least can take their time to turn them over, spell them out, examine them from the inside, give them a new twist, relate them to the lives and stories of women. This twisting and turning (and eventual unraveling) is the task I set myself when I sat down to write *The Hungry Self*, a book filled with perplexities and theories about the hunger of women.

Preface: The Hunger Knot

THIS IS A BOOK about women's entry into culture and society. As such, it could have been written about the contemporary struggle for a new, female identity without mentioning the current epidemic of eating disorders among women. But this is also a book about women and food, for a troubled relation to food is one of the principal ways the problems of female being come to expression in women's lives.

We must wonder, of course, why this is so. Why an obsession with food? And why now? Why do we find debilitating conflict when we might expect freedom and liberation? Why, in short, is there an epidemic suffering among women at this extraordinary moment when women are stepping out to claim a place for themselves in the world?

I am well aware that most people coming upon this book without preparation will be surprised to discover an association between eating and the struggle for identity. This sense of astonishment accompanied my own process of research and writing. My pages began to fill with references to the feminine mystique, the childhood struggle for identity, Marcel Proust's famous bite of Madeleine, the type of metaphor common to descriptions of religious experience, and the rites of initiation practiced in tribal societies. Indeed, these far-ranging associations presented themselves to me whenever I sat down to think or talk about women and food. Consequently, it has become my method in this apparent madness to claim for eating problems the same worth, seriousness, and distinction that compelled Freud, when writing about sexual problems, to evoke Oedipus and to support his findings about the universal nature' of the oedipal problem by a daring excursion into the totemic ritual of earliest tribal culture. Merely in associating sexuality and neurosis with the oldest stories and ritual of human beings, Freud implicitly established the historic importance of our sexual fantasies and the seriousness of what he believed was our culture's sexually originated, persistent malaise. Why not, therefore, use the same approach where eating is concerned?

The women whose stories appear in these pages came to speak with me about food. Many stayed to talk about their problems with love and work, their difficulties with their mothers and families, their dreams and aspirations, their incomplete and imperfect understanding of what it means to be a woman in our time. In presenting them I have, of course, taken pains to disguise them. Occasionally I have brought the stories of two women together and made a composite portrait that protects their identities and highlights the common themes of their lives. But their voices have been faithfully recorded so that they may speak here with the same urgency I first heard in my consultation room, where together we began to explore the unexpected meanings to which an obsession with food was leading us.

The topic of women and food—it is one of those marvelous, unraveling threads that can take us back to the origins of human culture, to the earliest experiences of every human life, through myth and rite and tale and fantasy, without ever departing from an essential relevance to contemporary women's lives. I therefore invite the reader, whether or not she is already fascinated by questions of childhood memory and tribal rite, to examine with me these troubled, tragic, and still unresolved developmental issues brought to our attention by eating problems.

Liberation from an obsession with food and weight takes place slowly and tends to move an individual through certain primary insights. These basic steps in understanding form the major sections of this book. For we are involved here in the same gradual process of decoding that informs the hours of conversation in a consultation room—peeling away surface appearances, the disguise of symptoms, and the confusion of compulsive behavior to reach the underlying meaning from which our liberation ultimately will arise.

To begin with, then, we will investigate the way a troubled relationship to food frequently hides a serious problem with female identity in an age when women are invited by social circumstance and individual inclination to extend the traditional idea of what it means to be a woman.

But this problem with female identity hides in turn a profound mother/daughter separation struggle, which becomes particularly acute when a daughter is required to surpass her mother. We can understand a great deal about this struggle by looking at the adult lives of mothers and daughters, but we shall also need to explore the roots of these adult conflicts and dilemmas that limit female development.

Consequently, the third step in this process requires us to explore childhood—to figure out how communication about identity takes place through food, to experience again how mother/daughter bonding is related to food, to examine hidden angers and needs and rages, and finally to understand the way food, in our adult lives, both leads us back to early childhood experiences and at the same time keeps us from reliving them.

Once this basic pattern has been grasped, we shall be able to see that the food obsession of contemporary women has all the elements of a rite of passage but that it fails to accomplish a rite's essential purpose—to move the individual from one stage in the life cycle to the next. Since neither the participants nor the healers in this collective ceremony fully understand what is being sought by the eating behavior, the obsession with food is split off from its true significance and therefore cannot serve to evolve a new type of female identity.

In the consultation room this pattern is never glimpsed as clearly as I have presented it. There, the precise order of insights and understandings can never be predicted. We move less often in a stage-to-stage progression, more frequently in a spiral, going in circles, meeting the same themes over and over again. But the process of understanding is basically the same: a question of correctly naming, stripping back, finding the roots, moving beyond that skein of impulse and inhibition, troubling fantasy, lost memory, and hidden desire that ties us to the past. This is the hunger knot, in which identity, the mother-separation struggle, love, rage, food, and the female body are all entangled. It is this we must unravel, patiently, meticulously, strand by strand, until we know ourselves.

I feel confident that a reader who follows me through the twists and turns of this discussion will be amply rewarded by her perseverance and that she will come, at the very least, to glimpse the possibility of transforming an obsession with food into an authentic ritual of transformation. Not that I mean to exclude men. There is much here that will serve to clarify their concerns with growth and development. But men tend to express their mother-separation struggle through a preoccupation with sexuality rather than eating. And my principal concern is with women and our struggle to claim a new female identity at this moment in history when we are for the first time in such large numbers creating our place in the world.

From the beginning, we must be aware of this crucial relationship between an eating obsession and that urgent moment in which women move into society and attempt the type of social and self-development we have, as a culture, more frequently assumed to be the privilege of men. Why the turmoil of this movement should come to expression in a disordered relation to food—that is one of the principal questions we must raise. For it shall become apparent that in raising the problem of an eating obsession we are opening a way into the most serious concerns of women's lives.

Indeed, we might go even further and assert boldly that an examination of our relation to food is the best possible way to discover the profound ambivalence and disguised guilt that are part of female self-development. It is in this sense precisely that our preoccupation with eating might well come to be that *royal road* to the unconscious that dreams proved to be for Freud. If this is true, we can understand our tendency to neglect and trivialize the psychological meanings in our eating behavior as a means of turning away from aspects of our emotional life we have not yet dared to confront. "I have an eating problem," we say, and we imagine that we are referring to a tormenting but circumscribed cluster of behaviors and attitudes. Yet, in reality, the moment we find the courage to look beyond the surface of this obsession, we come straight up against the most spiritual and political and deeply psychological issues that women face today.

I had originally intended to write only one book on the subject of women's obsession with food. I found, however, in the course of writing, that a single book could not adequately explore the theme of women's entry into culture. In *The Obsession* I present the issue of weight and body size as a cultural problem with female power. In the present book, I extend the analysis to include the mother/daughter bond and the issue of failed female development. In focusing my attention on the daughter's relationship to the mother, I do not mean to suggest that we can afford to slight the difficulties of the father/daughter bond in understanding either eating disorders or, more generally, the obstacles that arise when women claim power. Indeed, this theme of father/daughter confrontation will require a book in its own right and sufficient space to explore the relationship between eating obsessions and the prohibition against female creativity, which is common in a father-dominated culture. For that book, the next in the series, I shall take up the story of Eve in the Garden of Eden—a woman forbidden both food and knowledge by a father who claims to have created her without a female procreative counterpart.

My strategy here should be apparent. In all these books I wish to place women's struggle with food and eating within the largest possible context of meaning. We cannot heal ourselves until we understand the hidden struggle for self-development that eating disorders bring to expression in a covert way. We cannot indeed even begin to think about self-healing until we stop using the words "eating disorder" to hide from ourselves the formidable struggle for a self in which every woman suffering in her relationship to food is secretly engaged. We are a generation crossing over into the male sphere of self-development and social power. As a "generation" we include women of every age who undertake the struggle for a new sense of self. Women ten or twenty or forty years older than the adolescent girl afflicted with anorexia join this generation, regardless of age, if their anguish and need for a self, their aborted quest for identity, their need to undertake such a quest, make them unable to go on with life in the hallowed, traditional female ways. We are caught in a most serious dilemma, as we attempt to move beyond those revered notions that have always defined the "true nature of women." We are in trouble (and how else could it be, considering the magnitude of our task?) as we attempt to shape for ourselves a future unprecedented in what has been, indeed, until now, the history of man. Clearly, we need every bit of help and divine guidance and practical cunning we can find. For in our hands, these hands that lift children to our breasts and open books and pull us up unconquered mountains and cut wood and spice food and place that food in our mouths and in the mouths of our children, the future identity of generations of women is being prepared.

PART ONE

Identity

I

"I READ YOUR BOOK," she says. "I found . . . I found . . ."
She gives it up, shrugging. She looks helpless, as if it's already
clear she will not be able to express herself. But the silence is
making her uncomfortable. Now she breaks it with a rush of
words. "You're just like me, that's what I thought. Only, a
little bit ahead. You've suffered the same things, you know?
Running around eating, making yourself . . . get rid of it. But
you understand it. You have the answers . . ."

I don't think of myself as having the answers and I tell her so.

"What then?" She challenges me boldly, measuring me,
probably not aware how much hope and suspicion are in her
gaze.

"The right questions, maybe?"

She relaxes perceptibly, sitting back in the chair, but still on
guard, still cautious. But now she is smiling. "That's it?" she
says, mocking herself as much as me. "No cure, no therapy, no
answers? Just questions? I came here for more questions?"

Anita is a tall woman, with dark, exhausted, wary eyes. In
the weeks to follow, as she enters and leaves this room, I feel the
way she towers over me and I am aware how persistently she
hunches her shoulders and drops her head forward, whenever
she stands next to me. I am about to mention this to her, but
she, in a way I already recognize as typical, gets there first.

"Okay," she says one day when she walks into the room, "I know you've noticed it. I don't want to be bigger than you. I don't want to have answers you don't have. I don't even want to ask my own questions. Every time I think I'm getting a little bit ahead of you I draw back. I hesitate. I start to stutter."

She is a slender woman, with that gaunt, fashionable slenderness so popular today but not at all natural to her. Boyish, with short, feathered hair, she reminds me, in her running shorts and T-shirts, of a Greek youth, a young athlete in training. But she's a woman of almost forty and she leaves two preadolescent girls at home in the late afternoons when she jogs over to her appointment with me. She never comes late. When she sits down in the wicker chair, she apologizes for sweating. She apologizes for wanting a drink, for needing to use the toilet. She watches the time, leaping up a minute or two early to make sure she doesn't stay over.

"What's the hurry?" I say one day after we've been working together for several weeks.

"No rules here either?" she asks, with that air of ironic complicity that has charmed people all her life. "What happened to the rules? I suppose they went the same place as the cure? The therapy? The answers?"

But this possibility makes us both uneasy. There is no authority in this room, and we can't evade that. We're outside the defined, the authorized, the validated. We meet in my study, in the converted basement of my house, to see if we can figure out some way to articulate the questions that have not yet been answered by textbooks or the conventional therapeutic approaches. She's had, she tells me, on and off, close to fifteen years of therapy. She studied psychology in school. She's worked as a volunteer in a halfway house. Now her voice is growing bitter. And this, she says, is the first time she's admitted that she vomits four times a day, every day, and has done so since she decided ("Who knows why?") not to continue as a postdoctoral psychology intern more than eight years ago. We're in virgin territory. We struggle to define our own rules.

"What if I get in trouble and I want to call?"

"Well, what?"

"I guess I'm not supposed to?"

"Who made up that rule?"

"I *am* supposed to?"

"Who made up that one?"

She, who is quick to get the point, likes to prod and challenge until we arrive at it: she sits forward with a tight mouth, a grim expression, a jutting jaw, her elbows on her bony knees, blinking her eyes nervously. A fast talker, this one, rattling off the answers she's learned by heart, mocking them—the need for limits, the need to analyze the transference, the need for the therapist ("or whatever you call yourself") to remain a blank screen, to receive projections.

"Well," I say, "what if we put the whole question of rules aside and try to figure out what you're going to need, what I'm going to need, and see how it works out."

"I don't want to have needs," she blurts out, serious now. "And I don't want you to have them either."

Over the next weeks she tells the story of her life. Something about the shape of it has impressed me before now. "I suppose you've heard it all?" she asks. There are times, indeed, when she, with her unusual eloquence and the passionate outbursts to which she's subject, seems to be a generation's Speaker, leader of this choral anguish coming to expression now in women's lives.

"My mother was born in Panama," she says abruptly one day, "dark-skinned like me. A big woman, but we didn't think she was fat. Then, when we came here, she and my father and her sister and my father's sister—the whole family came—right away the four women went off and enrolled themselves in some diet group. That was what my father wanted. I was fourteen years old. My mother put me on a diet. We had a lot of money then. They bought me one of those bicycles you ride in the house. They converted the basement into a gym. They got one of those stationary running machines, a rubber tarp, one of those gadgets with belts for jiggling off fat. I was, at that point, taking after my mother. A big woman, but now we thought it was fat. And all this was part of the way she was preparing me to become an American, to take part in this society. I can't blame her. She wanted me to be a typical American girl. And that meant slender. And that meant diet. And that meant not cook or eat the way we ate in Panama. And that meant hectoring me. And that meant fights breaking out between us. And that meant, by the time I got to graduate school, I was a gymnast and a skier and a long-distance runner. I took diet pills to kill my appetite and keep me awake at night to study, and I kept it up until I got my doctorate. But then it was as if all those years of driving myself caught up with me. I started to lie around in bed and eat. I couldn't get up to go to work. Here I was, the fruit of all this discipline and hectoring and training, my family's pride, their ticket to the new world, a walking, talking American doll, a bit too tall, but just-right slender, and now I lay in bed and ate bags full of doughnuts, dozens of them, jelly-filled. And when I thought I'd burst from eating, and was terrified I wouldn't be able to stand up the next day and go back to the job, I went over to the toilet and taught myself how to vomit. Now that''—she goes on, through her tears, talking so fast I can barely understand her; she's reached out to clutch at my hand, and she squeezes it hard now—''that was a break-down. That wasn't an 'eating disorder' ''—the words stabbed out with contempt—''that was my life cracking apart. It was practically suicide.''

Identity

I've seen her face look bright and brittle, the way it was the first time she came in here; that smile, designed to hoodwink us all about her secret suffering. I've seen her look wary and suspicious, her eyes darting, her hands clenched nervously, the way she looked during our first hours of conversation. But this is the first time she's showed me that look of anguish. It ages her. For the first time I see lines in her face. Extraordinary, I think, that all this could be covered over by an act of will, a determination to seem perfectly normal, well-adjusted, content with her life.

"Why don't they know? Women are suffering. We're falling apart. But they don't get it. They just don't get it. They have the statistics, but they still don't understand. Even my father has the statistics. Last weekend, when the girls and I went home to visit, he's sitting in his chair after dinner when we're doing the dishes, and he reads bits of the paper to us if he thinks we'll be interested. 'You know what it says in the paper?' he asks. And then he tells us how many college women are suffering from bulimia. 'They throw up their food,' he says, shaking his head. 'Imagine that. They make themselves throw up their food.' 'Dad,' I wanted to scream at him. He sounded so smug, you know? 'Dad,' I wanted to shout, 'I'm one of them.'"

She interrupts herself. "Why don't I tell him? Is that what you're going to say? Oh, sure, tell him their precious Anita is falling apart? Can't stay in a relationship because she has to go out jogging every night after dinner after she's already vomited three or four times that day? Can't finish her clinical credential because she can't concentrate on the books? Too distracted by figuring out when she's going to binge the next time? You know, really, all someone would have to do to cure me of this obsession is to invent a machine I could tape over my stomach that would tell me exactly how many calories I've already eaten. Exactly how many—"

"We start out with the reason you can't talk to your parents about your life and we end up counting calories?"

"They want to believe it's all going just fine? They want to think I'm a little bit too thin and make a show of putting an extra piece of chicken on my plate? They want to believe I'll go back to my career as soon as my children are grown? That I'm staying home like my mother did, a necessary sacrifice for the children's sake? And I'm going to tell them the whole generation's gone mad?"

This woman does not think of herself as a feminist. She does not concern herself with the ERA or women's studies or rape crisis centers or abortion reform. She's not interested in women's literature. This is her own spontaneous urgency and anguish.

"I had a girl friend. On the day she was getting married she wouldn't come out of the room where she was dressing. It was late. She wouldn't talk to anyone. Finally, they got me and sent me in there. She opened the door. I took one look at her. Red eyes, that certain look in them. I knew she'd been vomiting. She said she couldn't go out there looking like that. She took a swig of some toilet water—you know, to hide the smell? And what was the whole thing about? She didn't want to marry that guy. And she couldn't tell them. She was engaged for a whole year and a half. Always pretending. You know what I think? That vomiting everyone says is so terrible? I think it was her only way out. That vomiting is some kind of scream of anguish. I think she was using that vomiting to let them know there was really something she just couldn't stomach."

"And you?"

"Sure. Okay. Me, too. I want them to know and not to know. But I just can't keep it in anymore. None of us can. We can't stomach it. We're vomiting our guts out to let them know we just can't stomach it."

"What can't you keep in anymore? What is it you just can't stomach?"

"There's something . . ." She puts her hand over her stomach; it's a strange gesture, the hand cupped protectively there, as if she were trying to keep something infinitely precious and valuable safe from harm. But at the same moment she's leaning forward, her face contorted, as if there's something she can't tolerate, something she wants violently to expel from herself. "Something awful . . . I can't say why. But at the same time—I don't know if I can explain this—but that awful thing is just something you can't do without. You can't give it up. But you just don't want to have it inside you."

This, I imagine, is what she must look like leaning over the toilet when she makes herself throw up, caught no doubt by this terrible ambivalence. But what is it, what is this thing she cannot tolerate and must get rid of at all costs, while at the same time trying to protect it?

"I'm telling you," she says, standing up to pace around and wave her arms. "I feel like I'm living with a seething mass in there." She's made her hands into fists and is pressing them against her stomach. "Sometimes it's a whirling thing, like a maelstrom, spinning and spinning and pulling me down into it. I feel like I could vomit for the rest of my life and I still wouldn't get rid of it. More would be there, it would be there and be there no matter what I did. But sometimes, after I spill out my guts and I have this first feeling of relief, I'm scared. I'm really frightened, suddenly. I break out in a sweat. What if I did something to harm myself, I think. What if I . . . what if I . . ."

She is standing a few inches from me, looking down at me with a desperate, harried expression, her eyes wide. "Why don't they know?" she says. "They talk and talk about vomiting. But they have no idea. This is my life. You see what I

mean? My whole life I'm choking on and spewing out and trying to gobble back again."

She takes a deep breath, casts one of those wary, frantic
glances at me. And now she turns and strides back and sits
down heavily in the chair. "It's . . . don't laugh." She
straightens herself up and looks at me with an expression I've
seen occasionally in the eyes of a woman driven finally to tell
the truth, however much it might embarrass her. "It's my life,
everything I am." She hesitates again, gathering herself. And
now it comes, in a choked, tentative voice. "It's my soul."

She is sobbing, her arms wrapped around her stomach, bent
over her knees. But she is still trying to talk, gasping for breath.
"This is what happens to me sometimes when I make myself
throw up. That's what I'm after. To feel . . . to feel terrible
even, to feel anything, to sob like this. I can't keep it in and I
can't get it out and I don't know what it is."

"It has something to do with your whole life, with everything
you are, with your dreams, with your soul?"

She nods her head, the crying muffled now, more like the
sobbing of a heartbroken child than that of an outraged, passionate woman. I wait, theories, interpretations rushing
through my mind. But we're not here to discuss theory. Not
yet. In her own way, I tell myself, she'll come to it. From
outburst to outburst. Piecing it all together. She has that type of
mind. First she pours it all out. Then she reflects on it. Constantly moving, from her experience and the stories she tells
about her friends to the accounts she reads and practically
memorizes from the newspapers and then back again to her
own anguish and suffering.

On the day after Karen Carpenter dies she comes in walking
fast, sits down, and leans toward me.

"Now they know," she says. "Now they'll have to take it seriously. It's all over now, we can't pretend anymore. Last night

Identity

I ripped her picture out of the paper and put it up on my bathroom door. And I promised myself. No matter what it takes. No more laxatives. No more vomiting. It's up to us now. We're the ones who still have a chance. If a hundred of us or even ten of us or even I just manage to stop now before it's too late . . ."

She shakes her head. "The waste. The awful waste."

II

WE ARE A UNIQUE generation of women—the first in history to have the social and psychological opportunity to surpass with ease the life choices our mothers have made. We come of age, we leave home, and we enter a world in which most social and political institutions have thrown open doors that for thousands of years were closed to women. Therefore, to many of us who have struggled for these very opportunities, it comes as a shock to realize that at that very moment when we might expect to step forward and harvest the fruit of a profound struggle for female liberation, many of the most gifted among us fall prey to a severe suffering that gradually consumes more and more of our life energy and finally causes what in many cases is a severe breakdown.

This crisis, in the form of serious and debilitating eating disorders, has received a great deal of recent attention in the national media, especially since the death of Karen Carpenter, the popular singer who died of a heart attack at the age of thirty-two, in a state of depletion caused by years of suffering from anorexia and bulimia. With her life and death, a generation of young women found their exemplar, the representative figure who spoke symbolically to their lives the way Janis Joplin had to the generation that came of age during the late 1960s.

For Karen Carpenter, in her struggle and suffering, was not

alone. In fact, there is, at present, a major epidemic of eating disorders in the United States. *The New York Times,* on July 14, 1982, reported that anorexia afflicts 1 in 250 girls between 16 and 18 years of age. Other estimates run as high as 1 in 100. Since less than 8 percent of all anorexics are male, we are forced to conclude that, in our time, eating disorders are a distinctive form of female suffering. But the statistics for bulimia (the syndrome in which periods of binge eating are followed by self-induced vomiting or the use of laxatives) are even more disturbing. According to the *San Francisco Chronicle* of October 31, 1982, 1 in 5 college-age women suffers from this severe disorder. Again, these figures may well be conservative estimates.

Indeed, since I first sat down to write these words some months ago, the statistics have become even more disturbing. "At least half the women on campus today suffer from some kind of eating disorder," says *Ms.* magazine, in an article surveying research in this field.

"The most dramatic finding," according to Michael G. Thompson, Ph.D., and Donald M. Schwartz, Ph.D., "was the prevalence of anorexic-like behaviors among normally functioning college women. These women were not impaired in their work, though they often felt that they were struggling. . . .

"The overall impression is of women—anorexic and anorexic-like and problem-free—experiencing their hunger as exaggerated and obscene, secretly wishing to gratify their impulse to eat, and constantly fighting this impulse."

But the newspaper articles and television specials have done little more than describe the "bizarre" symptomatology of eating disorders. We learn about the horrifying skeletal slenderness of a woman afflicted with anorexia. We hear about the thousands of calories consumed in a single binge, the hundreds of dollars spent on food that will be vomited up moments after having been consumed. There are even cases of women driven to prostitution or shoplifting to support their food habits. And there are of course numerous articles about the severe physical debilitation that can result from the various patterns of starving and gorging and purging. Teeth blacken and fall out, stomachs are ruptured, severe disturbances of electrolyte balance ensue. These shocking and disturbing details are reported over and over again. We hear less about the fact that the women involved in this troubled behavior often abandon their careers and their studies as the preoccupation with food takes over more and more of each of their lives. We are rarely told that they frequently return home, become extremely dependent on their parents, that their growth and development as human beings virtually comes to an end. We hear nothing at all about the relationship between the outbreak of eating disorders and the particular generation in which the women suffering from them have come of age.

I am reminded of Anita. There came a time, it was not long after our conversation, when the picture of Karen Carpenter, so desperately pinned up as admonishment, was taken down in a gesture of defeat. And then it was folded away in a notebook of memories, confessions, careful records of statistics, fragments of conversations between Anita and her friends ("I'm gathering evidence, the criminal evidence of what's happening these days to women's lives").

In the beginning it is enough to take the problem seriously, not to expect dramatic cures and radical solutions, to devote countless hours and days and weeks—the best of one's waking thoughts, the most careful record of one's nights of dreaming—to the task of understanding. I keep Anita in mind as I begin my work because she made me aware, as I never had been to that degree, just how much heroism a woman in our time needs if she is to ask certain basic questions about her life.

I remember her tendency to pit mind and passion, reason, will, feeling, and surmise against this other tendency we both have to move swiftly, to rush so fast one need not pause to reflect or ask for the meaning of one's behavior. Was I older than she, or younger, when I first knew that I could stop and wonder rather than act blindly? When did I first realize that it would not be the answers I gave that would bring me comfort, but this dogged, unrelenting, extremely stubborn, and by now persistent habit of asking questions?

Of course, it is never easy to say when exactly one first becomes aware of the real meaning in one's own struggle. I have been thinking about this problem of women and food for so many years now that I no longer find it easy to know exactly when my thinking first began. Years ago, it was my own rather desperate struggle not to run about and eat that first drove me toward consciousness. More recently, the many hours I spend speaking with women have augmented consciousness for me and given it a new shape, certain surprising twists and turns in its unfolding. But on reflection I find that there was a book, written by a woman, that helped me greatly during a difficult summer in my early twenties. As it happens, it was not a book about women and food. It did not come right out and tell me that an eating disorder was a serious form of identity crisis. But it scattered seeds, it turned my thinking in a particular direction, it set me dreaming and musing as I made my way through its pages. Reading it changed me in ways I would not then have been able to specify. But that is the way with reading. It gets in under the skin, and there, in darkness, it begins to prepare the work of fully conscious understanding. At the time, one reads and loses oneself in the reading and forgets to look up when the telephone rings, and one is transformed beyond one's wildest

hopes and imaginings by this act of slipping into the aching si-
lences of oneself, brought there by another woman's words.

In *The Feminine Mystique*, published in 1963, Betty Friedan
wrote about the "problem that has no name." She described
the lives of women who suffered from a feeling of emptiness,
rather than from the more easily identified distress that comes
from economic circumstance. I was far younger than most of
the women about whom she wrote. I had not made the conventional life choices they had made. But I knew that I, who suffered from an eating problem, also suffered from a feeling of
emptiness.

"The problem lay buried, unspoken for many years in the
minds of American women. It was a strange stirring, a sense of
dissatisfaction, a yearning that women suffered in the middle of
the twentieth century in the United States. Each suburban wife
struggled with it alone. As she made the beds, shopped for gro-
ceries, matched slip cover material, ate peanut butter sandwiches, chauffeured Cub Scouts and Brownies, lay beside her
husband at night, she was afraid to ask even of herself the silent
question: 'Is this all?' "

As Betty Friedan defined the problem, in a work that articulated for millions of American women the nature of their dilemma, this nameless suffering was a problem with identity, of
not knowing who or what one is or might wish to become. It
produced feelings of emptiness and incompletion, a desire to
run out of the house, to walk aimlessly through the streets, to
weep uncontrollably and for no apparent reason. There was a
feeling of desperation in these lives of affluent women living the
American dream, and a sense, too, of isolation and loneliness in
this suffering they hid from themselves and from others.

These feelings, Friedan came to believe, did not arise from
sexual repression, as most thinkers and analysts of her time
would have claimed. "It is my thesis that the core of the prob-

lem for women today is not sexual but a problem of identity—a stunting or evasion of growth that is perpetuated by the feminine mystique. It is my thesis that as the Victorian culture did not permit women to accept or gratify their basic sexual needs, our culture does not permit women to accept or gratify their basic need to grow and fulfill their potentialities as human beings, a need which is not solely defined by their sexual role.''

It is difficult in 1985 to experience the revolutionary and daring quality of this utterance. But these words, which two decades of feminist struggle have made it possible to take for granted, presented me with the missing key to my own locked suffering. I had grasped the idea that my problems with food were somehow related to a struggle for identity.

Today, I wish to suggest that the present epidemic of eating disorders must be understood as a profound developmental crisis in a generation of women still deeply confused, after two decades of struggle for female liberation, about what it means to be a woman in the modern world.

The suburban housewives Friedan described were a generation of women who had retreated from careers and professions, who closed themselves in the limited world of home and family, raised children, waxed floors, turned on the washing machine, drove children to schools and child-care centers, and tried to persuade themselves that they were fulfilled as mothers and housewives. It was these women, precisely, whose despair kept them awake at night as they struggled to deny their yearning for some larger destiny.

Therefore, it may seem paradoxical to suggest, as I am here, that now, when more women than ever before in the history of our land have returned to school, to meaningful professional work, to careers, and to their own creativity, there exists still a struggle to break free of that same feminine mystique that burdened women's lives a quarter of a century ago. Indeed, the struggle of women today may well be even more acute than that which was experienced twenty years ago. Certainly, the symptoms of our distress have become more extreme, the self-destruction more evident, the quality of crisis in the lives of women suffering from eating disorders even more violent and apparent.

Since Friedan wrote, the "silent question" has indeed become vocal. The problem without a name has been given a name. Women marching, women meeting together in small groups to discuss the hidden sufferings and sorrows of their lives, women discovering their literary and social heritage, in solitary acts of scholarship, in women's studies courses, publishing, discussing, disputing, organizing, women raising their children in new ways, confronting husbands, families, social institutions, have been naming their conditions, analyzing the circumstances that give rise to them, and answering the silent question with a resonant *no*. No, we say, this is not all. The lives of women are larger, we insist, than we have been told they may be. We are the generation seeking to establish this truth before history, in the eyes of the world. If, therefore, we are still struggling with questions of identity—at a time when we are conscious of having a new identity as women, of having the right to this identity and the right even, in some cases, to luxuriate in this accomplishment—the whole question of identity must be even more complex and problematic for women than we have supposed.

It may be that this problem that had no name and has since been called a struggle for identity has once again become hidden and silent. Or perhaps it has taken on a false, misleading name, so that we no longer recognize the old problem with identity in its new guise? We write countless articles, interview great numbers of women, describe their suffering with a food obsession, gather statistics, open centers, cite experts, and evolve various approaches to treating eating disorders. But we apparently do not yet associate them with the historic moment in which women, after thousands of years of suppression, enter the world.

There is something eluding us here about our struggle; something hidden, something secret, something ignored by all our explanations. Left in shadow, it must continue to cause the severe debilitation and crisis we observe today. Women suffering from eating disorders are telling us, in the only way they know how, that something is going seriously wrong with their lives as they take on the rights and prerogatives of male society.

III

IT REQUIRES, OF COURSE, a leap of imagination to associate the self-starvation of a woman, or the consumption of three pounds of chocolate, or the use of 144 laxatives a day, with the struggle for new female identity. And yet, women describing their own condition frequently make a spontaneous association between questions of identity and eating problems. The novelist Kathryn Marshall, in an article for *Savvy* magazine, describes this relation in the following way: "I was no longer a dancer; no longer a paradigm for . . . the sexually desirable female. I was no longer a bona fide sylph. *And I had no bona fide self.* [Emphasis added.] What I did have was a troubling obsession with bingeing and vomiting."

One characteristic of this lack of a "bona fide self" is that same feeling of emptiness Friedan found in women's lives. "There is no I," says a woman in her late twenties. "There's just an immense hole at the center. An emptiness. A terror. Not all the food in the world could fill it. But, I try."

In my work with women who experience despair and conflict in their relation to food, I have found that in the first hour they talk about eating. By the second or third hour they tell me they feel confused and do not know what to do with their lives. They have little sense of who they are or what they believe. They are lost, empty, restless, confused, and dissatisfied. They are struggling with all the questions of identity their mothers also faced.

A generation ago, Betty Friedan asked: "What if the terror a girl faces at twenty-one, when she must decide who she will be, is simply the terror of growing up—growing up, as women were not permitted to grow before? What if the terror a girl faces at twenty-one is the terror of freedom to decide her own life, with no one to order which path she will take, the freedom and the necessity to take paths women before were not able to take? What if those who choose the path of 'feminine adjustment'—evading this terror by marrying at eighteen, losing themselves in having babies and the details of housekeeping—are simply refusing to grow up, to face the question of their own identity?"

It is clear that far fewer women today retreat into marriage and housekeeping as a means of evading the terror of self-development. Indeed, in the last two decades we have been observing the opposite movement, away from the home and family. And yet it is beginning to seem apparent that this same terror of female development is evident in a new form even among women who succeed, externally, in making this movement back to the world.

An eating disorder is, in fact, an extremely effective way to stop the movement into the world. In severe cases it brings development completely to an end as the woman retreats from social life, from classes, from all other interests and occupations to spend her days poring over calorie charts, weighing chicken breasts ("broiled, not sautéed, not ever sautéed"), measuring waist and ankles and thighs, frantically running or taking long, joyless walks. ("Some days, even in the rain, I walk thirty, forty miles. What difference does it make? I've given up all other activity anyway.")

If we listen to women who suffer from this affliction, we will find that they are frequently telling us exactly what they are suffering from, even when they themselves do not understand the full range of implications. Recently, in the *San Francisco Chronicle,* there was a story about Debbie, a twenty-three-year-old student at Santa Clara, who had suffered from bulimia for two years. During that time she lost a great deal of weight, dropped out of school, moved back home to live with her family, took 144 laxatives a day, ate in secret, spent entire days planning her eating and vomiting, finally overdosed on medications, and awoke in a hospital, "where nurses and her parents were yelling at her." Her suicide attempt took place on the eve of her sister's wedding. And she, reflecting about her life, says, "My whole identity was placed on my weight."

An identity crisis, says Erik Erikson, one of the leading figures in the field of psychoanalysis, "is now being accepted as designating a necessary turning point, a crucial moment, when development must move one way or another, marshalling resources of growth, recovery and further differentiation." Clearly, then, when an eating disorder develops at what might otherwise be a turning point in a woman's life, this marshaling of resources for growth is not taking place. Instead of freedom and liberation we find obsession, and in it the underlying quest for identity and development is drowned.

Psychology is intended to serve the cause of human freedom. By entering into the shadows that surround our conscious knowledge of ourselves, we hope to liberate our capacities for joy, for growth, for development, for the full exercise of all the latent powers and potentials that lie buried or knotted within us. Erikson has little to say about the distinctive crises through which women, as distinctive beings, inevitably pass as we move out into the world. There is a missing chapter in our understanding. And we, the women who undertake this movement into social power, must begin from our new knowledge of ourselves to write that text. So much still missing, so much we scarcely dare yet know, so many conflicts and themes not yet sounded in the annals of human introspection. It is an awesome task, this quest for consciousness, and not the least of the challenges presently confronting us.

In my own work it has become clear to me that the onset of an eating disorder coincides with an underlying developmental crisis, regardless of a woman's age. For age is simply not the relevant factor in an eating problem. Today, the obsessions with food, the control of the appetite, and the size of the body have begun to involve women of every age. In a survey conducted in 1981 by the National Association of Anorexia Nervosa and Associated Disorders, 25 percent of 1,400 respondents who diagnosed themselves as having anorexia or bulimia were older than thirty. On reflection, the reason for this is clear. As a culture, we increasingly offer the struggle for development and new identity to women at stages of life when past generations would have expected them to decline mutely into middle age. Among us, women of all ages return to school, open a business, take up the long-abandoned desire for creative expression, or involve themselves in serious political and spiritual work. In doing so they significantly change their relation to their family, their past, and the concept of self they have had throughout their lives.

Indeed, at times this struggle for new identity may remain entirely hidden from the woman herself until she begins to explore an eating problem that is covertly bringing her longing to expression. She may, for instance, be a person who has lived her whole life in a deep and evident concern for the people around her. And now, while her children are not yet fully grown, she suddenly finds herself eating compulsively and disliking her large body, which she had accepted for years.

"I always thought of myself as having ten breasts," a woman

tells me, in her characteristically vivid way. "One for every member of the family. And a few left over for the neighborhood." But now, she admits, she has begun to feel that "something is eating" at her.

"Really," she says, putting her hand on her stomach, "I can feel it right here, gnawing away."

"Well," I say, "if it's eating away at you, maybe that's because you don't know what else to feed it."

She roars with laughter. "It's sure not satisfied with chocolate pudding anymore."

I wait a moment and then I ask: "So, what is it you want more than anything in the world?"

She gives me a quick, deep look, trying, I think, to figure out whether she can trust me with her secret. And then, finally, turning her head slightly away in a self-protective gesture, she confesses: "I want to write poetry."

We might not guess that the desire to write poetry could drive a woman into disturbing episodes of compulsive eating, in the hope that she might fill an ill-defined "gnawing hunger" whose real nature she cannot admit to herself. But in fact the desire to write must inevitably produce significant upheaval in this woman of the ten breasts, who has experienced her entire life as if she were the "great earth mother," put down here to "feed the world." If she is to write poetry, she must come to believe that she has something to say, a right to take time from her family in order to say it, and even a right to that room of her own Virginia Woolf found so essential to creative endeavor. These things are formidable achievements for anyone. Indeed, a woman who succeeds in granting herself these rights may be well on her way to writing poetry successfully. After that, the struggle with language is definitely a lesser battle.

Middle-aged mothers and their adolescent daughters who are leaving home frequently find themselves in similar positions: both face a demanding social reality that invites them to dare what few generations of women have ever dreamed to undertake. The woman of eighty who joins the Gray Panthers or begins to distribute literature to promote the rights of senior citizens faces the same potential confrontations as her granddaughter who is leaving for college at the end of the summer. Therefore, it seems at the very least suggestive to imagine that the epidemic nature of eating problems among us is telling us two things. On the one hand, we can no longer simply swallow the "hungers" and ambitions women have traditionally distanced from themselves. On the other hand, we are profoundly agitated by the "appetites" that have erupted within us. We are in conflict, and so far, as a generation, we have expressed this uncertainty about who we are and what we may become through the disturbing symptomatology of eating disorders.

Older women rarely think of themselves as being in the grips of a fierce struggle and conflict over identity. They are astonished and ashamed to find that, after a lifetime of dwelling in a particular body, with a more or less tolerable relation to food, they are suddenly invaded by nameless urges and desires and by a restless sense of self-contempt.

Here is the way one woman with an unusual capacity for self-reflection speaks about the discovery that her obsession with food and weight arose at a transitional moment in her life. Her musing will allow us to glimpse one reason a woman today might develop a serious eating disorder while twenty years ago women, although they ate and grew heavy, did not become obsessed with their eating and did not follow out this obsession into severe, self-destructive behavior.

"I know all about filling emptiness with food," she says, leaning back in her chair, her hands clasped behind her head as she sighs and smiles and looks over at me with a knowing glance.

"First, of course, you can fill it by making food for other people. I was always good at that. And it gave me a good excuse to eat, sometimes a whole loaf of bread, slice by cooling slice, not at all compulsively, calmly, with a thick layer of butter and jam, and then even to begin on the second loaf, interrupted only because the children have come home from school. No problem if I went from a size-sixteen apron to a size-eighteen sack. I could, after all, wear my size-twenty coat down to the supermarket for my day's excursion, couldn't I?"

The woman who is telling me this story is a large woman. She has, however, exchanged that size-eighteen sack for "ample tailored garments," as she describes them. She is sitting forward more urgently now, her arms folded on the well-endowed bosoms she refers to, in a self-mocking voice, as her "divine apportionment."

Several years ago she became the director of an employment agency that seeks jobs and career training for minority women, and she turns now less often this gift of the telling phrase against herself.

But this is how she describes, with typical verve, the day she stood reflecting on her life at a moment of developmental urgency. For almost an hour, she says, she found herself in front of a large mirror before a closet filled with "garments of shame—the draped and the drab," she calls them, clothes right for the neighborhood kaffeeklatsch, but unsuitable for a first meeting with the women's dean.

"Would you believe it? I never gave the girth a single moment's thought. I ate, I called myself zaftig, not fat. My husband likes a 'generous woman.' And of course for the children a mother is always the most beautiful woman in the world. I lived, you know how: from morning to midnight it was hand to mouth. Hand in the cookie jar, hand in the mouth. And what did it matter if I was staying at home? But the first day I had an appointment to talk with a professional woman about the rest of my life, suddenly I'm not zaftig anymore, in my sacks and moomoos. I'm fat suddenly, I'm inappropriate, I'm grotesque.

"Later, I could look back; later, I could see, of course I was feeling unsure of myself, I felt inadequate, I didn't think I belonged out there. How does a fat woman of fifty-five go talk with the Dean of Women, who is half her age, slim and tailored, and at ease with her life? Today, yes, today I can say it was the self-doubt and uncertainty about myself that made me, after a lifetime of body-tolerance, suddenly call myself fat. But at the time my only thought was, 'Sally, get yourself on a diet.' That day, I actually canceled the appointment. I put it off until I could lose weight. You know what happened to me? A familiar story? I lost my weight. But by then I had the eating problem. I didn't vomit or use laxatives or starve myself. But my mind was so filled with the counting of calories that by the time I finally went to enroll in graduate school how could I concentrate on any other work?''

IV

THE WOMAN WHO REMAINS at home succeeds in hiding from the fundamental issues of female development. Filling her sense of incomplete and inadequate self-development with food, she makes use of the traditional expectation that she nourish others to bury her own nagging sense of emptiness. The size-sixteen apron hides both the restless hungers that are troubling her and the problems her body will cause for her once she decides to strip away the apron's protective domestic armor and take her large body, with all its appetites, out into the world. For then the inner turbulence that has long been denied breaks through and comes to the surface as an acute distress, a profound sense of self-dissatisfaction and low self-esteem. She hates her body, she finds it grotesque. She has spent most of her adult life hiding from the truth of her life. She opens the door, steps out into culture, and her crisis overwhelms her.

This hiding from the stark truth of one's condition as a woman occurs also among women far younger who, with apparent ease, are crossing over into culture. In 1983, young feminists speak from the pages of *Ms.* magazine and insist that they have solved the issues of identity Betty Friedan raised twenty years ago on behalf of their mothers.

"My friends and I," writes Naomi Wolf, "are the first women in history who were brought up to take access into any institution as a given: if we were good enough, we were told, it would be ours—and astonishingly, up through the rarified competitive arena of a university like Yale it is.''

In an eloquent and vivid essay, this young writer describes her experience in this new world for which an earlier generation struggled. ''I think of the telling of women's history and the shaping of a female criticism as one of the great scholarly tasks of the next century, and I'm not alone: every paper we write on Anglo-Saxon women healers or the fear of the female poet in Spenser feels like a reclamation, a deep-sea dive in which we come up saying, 'This is mine.' When I meet with my professor on autumn afternoons in her book-lined study with the sun slanting through the panes, admiring the beautiful age on her face and listening to her voice's cadence as she illuminates Chaucer, I can think, I want to grow old like that; she can think, Here is a young woman to whom what I give is precious.''

It is difficult to read these words without being moved. Here, on this autumn afternoon, in the book-lined study, between these two women, teacher and student, so much that we have struggled for finds it consummation. Whatever questions these two women ask together, about Spenser and women healers, they would seem no longer to concern themselves with the silent question to which Betty Friedan gave voice. Their lives are its answer: they have entered that larger life their own mothers no doubt so poignantly and bitterly lacked.

And yet . . .

I hesitate to cast the least shadow upon this moment of fulfillment and quiet contentment between women. And I hasten to add that it remains real and valid and essential in spite of what I am going to say next. But I am aware that even as these two women sit together in the book-lined study, all around them, on that very campus where they are working, in restaurants and in apartments and in dorms, other women, in alarming numbers, are consuming packages of M&Ms, boxes of granola cereal, countless ice cream sandwiches and numberless chocolate cookies and then rushing into the bathroom, where they gulp down glasses of water to help themselves vomit.

And yet, none of the young feminists writing in *Ms.* mention the fact that on the campus around her some 50 percent of her female classmates are involving themselves in behavior that threatens their social adjustment, their most intimate relationships, their struggle for self-development, and in a significant number of cases even their lives.

There is a disturbing distance here between the idea of ourselves we wish to hold and the predicament with which our actual behavior confronts us.

Another young woman, of the same generation as Naomi Wolf, sent me this description of a typical day in her life when she was a college student.

> *She knew what she had to do before it was too late, and she rose up with difficulty and walked across the thick carpet to the bathroom, and flicked on the light. The tiled floor was cold under her bare feet. She shivered slightly and turned to face the mirror above the sink as she pulled back her long hair and fastened it with a rubber band.*
>
> *Then she turned on the faucet, full force, and filled a glass of water. She left the water running out of habit, though this time it wasn't necessary since no one was around to hear the sounds from the bathroom. When she had finished the glass of water she lifted the lid of the toilet and knelt down before it, her face within the bowl. She pushed her finger down on the back of her tongue in the exact right spot and the brownish liquid gushed out of her.*

It is essential that we hold these two images in our minds simultaneously—the autumnal portrait of the two women at work together in the book-lined study discussing Spenser and the picture of the young woman gagging and vomiting, by choice, into the toilet bowl. It is in the meeting of these two images that we shall come to understand the dilemma of women alive in the world today.

For the woman vomiting and for an epidemic number of her sisters, the question of female identity, even now that it has become vocal, has not been laid to rest. For in this proud, assertive, forgivably arrogant generation of women, on behalf of which Naomi Wolf expresses herself ("Our luxury then is to be able to get on with the work"), countless women simply cannot allow themselves an affirmative response to the new conditions of social, political, and institutional freedom offered to women for the first time, to this degree, in the history of the world.

"When I got to college," writes Diane Salvatore, another young feminist speaking out from the pages of *Ms.*, "I thought the world had been through everything. . . . Nothing could possibly shock. We could be any kind of women we wanted to be. Instead, for many, it was a classic case of sensory overload. With too many options, we panicked and retreated into old roles or new apathy, one that took for granted too many freedoms and said things like 'Everyone is basically bisexual'; 'I'm going to earn $45,000 by the time I'm thirty'; 'Of course I'll get into med school'—without acting on them, or, I suspect, really understanding them."

For thousands of years we have been that half of humanity struggling to content ourselves with lives of sacrifice and struggle, telling ourselves God wanted it that way, the pain even of birthing a child, the sacrifices involved, the submission to domestic ideology. And then suddenly, within a generation, we are invited to take for granted entry into medical school, the ability to climb Annapurna, the possibility of climbing up the corporate ladder along with the men, wearing pants just like theirs and suits cut in the sharp edge of the highest masculine fashion, without needing to remember that women were insulted and abused, some fifty years before, when they wore bloomers in public. Perhaps we take it for granted, today, that we can speak out on the floor of Congress, at the school board, in the Supreme Court, without needing to remind ourselves that when Susan B. Anthony and Elizabeth Cady Stanton traveled the roads of Kansas and California, struggling to win the vote for women, they were "pelted by rotten eggs and vegetables." Perhaps we no longer hear the echo of that outraged mob jeering at Emma Goldman when she spoke out against conscription, shouting: "strip her naked" and "tear out her guts." Or perhaps these echoes from history endure; perhaps they have entered so deeply into the fabric of our mind and being that they sound in our ears even today, the silent background to the silent question about the legitimacy of female development. After all, the angry shouting of the mob and the hushed question scarcely able to speak itself out when the woman lies awake in bed at night have had thousands and thousands of years to gather force.

"I believe nothing has been as damaging to women," Gerda Lerner writes in the summer 1983 issue of the *Women's Studies Quarterly,* "as 5000 years of systematic deprivation from access to knowledge and from participation in the formation of philosophies which explain the world to us and from the religions which shape our emotions and values."

We have been seriously harmed during the last millennia and we now must become conscious of the precise forms this harm has taken. The widespread suffering among women today, for which we have no good explanation, no deep and meaningful healing, suggests that we are in grave danger of simplifying the whole question of what it means for a generation of women to take upon their own shoulders this difficult task of entering a world that has refused to see us as human beings with the same crises of development that have received thousands of years of expression on behalf of men.

And so we leave home, we leave the apron and the sack dress behind, we put on blue collars and hard hats and tailored executive suits. We roll up our shirt-sleeves as the boys do and settle in to work in their sphere, where certain qualities are admired, other traits abhored. We are sensitive to these distinctions—newcomers always are. We keep our eyes open, our ears take in subtle communications a more secure person could afford to miss. And now we take ourselves in hand, tailoring ourselves to the specifications of this world we are so eager to enter. We strip our bodies of flesh, our hearts of the overflow of feeling, our language of exuberant and dramatic imprecisions. We cut back the flight of our fancy, make our thought rigorous and subject it (this marvelous rushing intuitive leaping capacity of ours) to measures of demonstration and proof, trying not to talk with our hands, trying hard to subdue our voices, getting our bursts of laughter under control.

Feeling the weight of these long years of exclusion, are we inclined to evade the whole question of the distinctive forms female development must take? Will we instead simply dress and shape ourselves like men, assume their attributes and qualities and thereby avoid the years of experimentation, struggle, trial, and effort necessarily involved in this immense task of creating ourselves?

Generations of immigrants have done it before us. Generations of ethnic minorities have changed language, style of dress, and manner of expression to get into that exclusionary society of power and privilege. Women are the new immigrants crossing the border from an old world. And meanwhile, as we make ourselves over into men, we are busily stripping ourselves of everything we have been traditionally as women.

Recently, I have been thumbing through magazines looking for indications of this dilemma. (It is possible to read a popular magazine with the same attention to symbolic undertone and resonant detail we bring to a work of literature.) I have found that the tendency, observable during the last decade at least, for female clothes to imitate male fashion has progressed. We no longer need to interpret the styles. Very boldly now, they show their true colors.

Thus, in the October 1983 issue of *Self* magazine we are shown a picture of a young woman in black-striped pants, wool jacket, and silk shirt wearing wing-tipped shoes. "The look," says the accompanying text, "might have been borrowed from a man (more likely: an Eton schoolboy), but the clothes are all from Perry Ellis's women's collection—a lesson in the men's-look potential your own closet may already have."

Next the article goes on frankly to discuss the way traditional manufacturers of male attire have begun to make men's clothes for women. "If you thought menswear-for-women had reached its limits with the boxer shorts a page back, who could fault you?" the writer asks. And then she tells us that Jockey International has made a male undershirt for women, that Calvin Klein is about to release "bikinis and tanks cut like a man's briefs and undershirts," and that therefore American women are finding themselves "dressing all the way down to the skin in menswear."

This article is worth reading slowly. Brooke Shields, the model, is described as "the latest in the current string of stars to cross-dress on film: You can glimpse Brooke-as-a-boy in *Sahara,*" the article says, making it very clear that the issue of female identity is at stake here and that we are, as a generation, seriously experimenting with the possibilities of being men. "Dressing like a man doesn't mean you want to be a man," the writer assures us. But I wonder. In the final portrait of Brooke-as-boy, we see her in clothes clearly too large for her, not at all cut to provide that "contrast of a woman's curves" the other pictures claim to demonstrate. Here, Brooke looks for all the world like a little girl dressed up for a masquerade party in an older brother's clothes. Curves have vanished. The woman herself, as woman, has vanished. And now, to be sure, the text tells us that "instead of dressing *like* a man," we might "try actually dressing in men's clothing." We are encouraged "not to take fit too seriously," just to "roll, belt, cuff and relax."

The question of "fit," however, is important. Rolling, belting, cuffing, and relaxing are simply not adequate to the imperative task of creating an identity that "fits" us as we enter the world. If we interpret these sartorial symbolisms as statements about the way we are struggling for identity, we can see just how far we still are from evolving an attire that could bring to expression our unique female possibilities.

"You may be a banker by day. But you're a woman by night," says the advertisement. The page shows a woman divided. Tailored, hair tucked up, hand in pocket, chin lifted, shoulders straight, somewhat reserved, definitely dignified and rather aloof, she stands there on the left-hand side of the page in her banker's clothes. In the larger picture on the right-hand side we see the same woman in her boudoir, hair down around her shoulders, hand to chin, soft and seductive and "sensuous" in her Kayser gown. But why do they imagine this advertisement would appeal to women of our time? Are they right? Are we willing to accept this distinction that clothes us like men when we are in the man's world and strips us back to our "essential femininity" for them in bed at night? And suppose the woman needed to be reserved and dignified and straight-shouldered in the nightgown and soft and sensuous in her business garb. Would that make her a woman by day and a banker by night?

The struggle is difficult. How could it be easy to find a way to cherish, perhaps even to evolve qualities that have always been despised in women and to bring them boldly into a culture that cannot yet ratify the Equal Rights Amendment? No doubt it seems easier simply to clothe ourselves in the male attire that stands for privilege and power. Looking through these pages, one is reminded of a shaman covering himself in the skin of an animal whose qualities and attributes he wishes to assume. But for women today the taking on of male qualities, and male fashions, is extremely problematic, particularly at a time when we are suffering from an inadequate knowledge of how women, as women, are to make their way in this masculine world. If tight dresses and seductive clothes or the frilly fashions of little girls are no longer appropriate to us, surely this does not mean our only alternative is to dress ourselves like men and to accept this sharp and terrible self-division?

We must not, at all costs, slight the magnitude of our dilemma, even when an anxiety about the appropriate forms of female development, and the feared sacrifices and losses involved in it, speak to us from the fashion pages of popular magazines. Whether we are being permitted (and encouraged) to dress as men or soothed in our anxiety about losing our femininity, these pages reflect conflicts and preoccupations we are not yet able to discuss in any other form.

Our obsession with losing weight and keeping ourselves small, our determination to remake the female body so that it suits masculine attire, our retreat into the masculine exterior disguise, our desperate eating of large amounts of food, our starvation of ourselves, our forced purges and evacuations of the food we take into ourselves—they all express the immense burden of female self-development. Eating disorders express our uncertainties, our buried anguish, our unconfessed confusion of identity. So far, in our struggle for liberation, we have become women dressed in male attire and not yet, by any means, women clothed in the full potential of female being.

For there is, in our resistance to being female, something far more disturbing than the penis envy Freud suggested, far less biologically determined and far more culturally imposed— something that every woman faces when she seeks her own development and that no man must ever face. Indeed, the problem with female identity that most troubles us, and that is most disguised by our preoccupation with eating and body-size and clothes, has a great deal to do with being a daughter and knowing that one's life as a woman must inevitably reflect on the life of one's mother. This is the anxiety that makes us yearn to wear male clothes, regardless of fit, and to work over and worry at and reshape these female bodies of ours so that they can help us pretend we have managed to escape from being our mothers' daughters and have, in our appearance at least, become their sons. Our mothers' sons—those being for whom self-development and the struggle for identity are an entirely legitimate enterprise.

PART TWO

Daughters and Mothers

I

She pulled back the covers and crawled into the bed. One piece of chocolate wouldn't hurt. Just one tiny piece. She deserved that much, she had been so good. (You'll get fat.) Not with just one. She could see them there in the closed box, tiny jewels laid out in rows. Ripping off the gold paper, she lifted the lid and there they were; square ones, oval ones, round ones with almonds on top. Hers to choose.

(You'll get fat!) What difference did it make? She bit into the first piece, a caramel melting with chocolate, and she allowed the hunger to rise as she ate mouthful after mouthful. Chewy, sweet, chocolaty. Eating faster, more, she licked her fingers when the last one was gone and lay back on the pillows feeling her distended belly with her sticky fingers.

(You're a bad, bad, bad, bad girl! You know what will happen to you, little girl? You'll get fatter and fatter and fatter. Until your body bloats out like the women in the "before" pictures in the newspaper ads. Like your mother. Like your fat aunt. Like your sister! Look what happened to them. They all used to be so slim and ambitious. Then they got married and had babies. Look at them now! Your mother so ashamed she never leaves the house. You're a fat little piggy. Bad, bad, bad.) [From "The Hunger" by Kimberly Kluger-Bell]

It is worth considering the fact that for most women the new image of female development is not handed down by a mother. It is worth considering what it means to a woman putting food into her mouth that she must immediately fear this food will turn her into a woman whose life is without ambition, who married and had babies and feels so ashamed that she does not dare to leave her house. For a daughter whose mother's life has made this impression on her, the act of eating will be fraught with peril. With every bite she has to fear that she may become what her mother has been. For here is a woman who cannot receive directly from her mother, as part of the mother's dream of succession, the privilege of self-development. She cannot take as a personal inheritance those years of wisdom and study the professor in the book-lined study is handing down. A handful of cherished recipes, perhaps, a lifetime of broken dreams and disillusion—that is what most women alive today can receive from their mothers. We are a generation who, with every act of self-assertion as women, with every movement into self-development and fulfillment, call into question the values by which our mothers have tried to live.

For Friedan, it was the absence of a private image telling a woman "who she is, or can be, or wants to be" that accounted for the inability to resist the "feminine mystique." Poignantly, she describes the women who could not see themselves beyond the age of twenty-one, girls afraid to grow up because they had no image of possibility for a woman.

But this absence of imagery can no longer account for identity problems or for the terror women feel when facing the demands of self-development. We know by now what women can be. We have begun to uncover our buried literature and restore the history of our participation in the world. What is it, then, that creates such serious identity conflicts for a woman today? What could it be that drives a young woman of college age, or an older woman returning to college, to gather all her will, her discipline, her energy around the weighing out of a piece of meat, stripped of its fat, carefully cooked without oil, when for the first time in history the college she is attending has appointed a woman to a tenured chair? Why indeed should a woman of any age spend one hundred dollars a day for food she's going to make herself vomit up within half an hour of eating it, drop out of the graduate program to which she has so recently returned because she cannot afford this practice, and then, as part of her retreat from her own development, spend her days selling fish and chips in front of the same highly prestigious college of which her own mother, raised in the mountains of Tennessee, had not even heard?

At a moment when serious political gains have been won and women are able to take up the opportunity for further development, there is a marked tendency among women to retreat, to experience a failure of nerve, a debilitating inner conflict about accepting advantages and opportunities denied to their mothers. The "Cinderella complex," the fear of independence from which we are supposedly suffering, is in reality a pervasive worry about our mothers' lives.

This anguished concern about the mother is hidden just beneath the surface of the eating problem. If we are to understand the contemporary struggle for female identity, we must place it in relation to this fateful encounter between a mother whose life has not been fulfilled and a daughter now presented with the opportunity for fulfillment.

These mothers call me, seeking help and guidance for daughters who were, as they say, "in the pink of health," "blossoming," "the ideal adolescent; she didn't take drugs, she didn't smoke or drink; she was a cheerleader, she got good grades." "Have I done this to her?" they ask a stranger over the telephone. "We were a perfect family," they say, sighing bitterly. "Was that the problem? We didn't prepare her to venture out into this world?"

I, who spend many hours each day with the daughters, put down the phone and sit for a long time in silence at my desk. Each day I see, more and more clearly, how deeply these two women, mother and child, are caught by this new generation's daring, its refusal of the past, its rejection of all those sacred ideals concerning womanhood—and above all by its refusal of the self-sacrifice involved in mothering.

For the older woman, what terrible sorrow there must be. Her life has gone by. It is too late, she thinks, to do all those things about which this young girl, with her fresh face and eager expectations, rushes home to tell her. And so we imagine that the daughter finds her mother standing in the kitchen. She knows, this mother of the 1980s, that no one any longer values much the care she gives to the preparation of the family meals. And yet, in that quarter-hour before her adolescent daughter entered the room, she had been wondering what new form to give the food she serves up, so dutifully, each night. She looks up, this woman in her fifties, who weighs ten or fifteen pounds more than she wishes to. She wipes her hands on her apron. She lifts a hand to tuck back a straying wisp of hair, remembering this same moment in her own life twenty-five years earlier. And did she go to college? Did she have her pick of the finest universities in the land? Did she go there to get a husband? Or because, as this girl claims, the digging up of ancient cities presses upon her with a restless lure? She does not want money, this daughter who has known every privilege. She does not want to marry, she says, and have children, until she has lived. And what is life, then, the mother asks, trying to keep that edge out of her voice? Are you telling me, she wonders, falling silent, pressing her lips closed, are you telling me that my life of sacrifice and devotion was not living at all?

Daughters and Mothers

For the daughter (or the woman of any age coming of age in this new way we now invite women to develop), the confrontation with the despairs and failures of the mother's life must inevitably produce a feeling of profound dismay. Any one of us could surround ourselves with pictures of Emma Goldman or Fannie Lou Hamer or Radclyffe Hall or Margaret Sanger made abundantly available in popular women's magazines and derive from them all the sustenance and encouragement our mothers lacked. But the fact that few women of any age fill their homes with this iconography may have something to do with the battle of opposing imagery that faces us today. The dominant image for the woman vomiting is not the image of Fannie Lou Hamer, the black activist who struggled for her people's right to vote; for the woman getting into bed to devour chocolates it is not the image of Margaret Sanger conquering fear by crossing the railroad tracks alone. For the woman vomiting it is the image of a fat mother hiding at home, a sacrifice to an earlier generation's conception of motherhood and appropriate female destiny, that dominates her imaginary life.

If it is true that our mothers in their time suffered from a lack of imagery and were severely limited in their development because of this, we their daughters suffer from an acute, unnamed conflict between the image of mother we carry as a restless inheritance and the new image of female possibility our time presents. Here, precisely, is a piece of the missing chapter we need to write. For here is a feeling so bitter in its implications few of us have been able to become aware of it. Imagine a woman stepping out joyfully into her own new life who now feels herself torn between her loyalty to her mother and her response to that new woman, that new female being we are all struggling toward. Of course, she cannot go back to being what her mother was, but we can imagine how this inability must fill her with remorse.

And so we behold them, the women of our time, mother and daughter both caught in this dilemma: the mother lifting the telephone to call a stranger who may be able to help her with this beloved daughter who has returned from school and who sits grimly at the family table during meals, rushing off to vomit afterward or surreptitiously hiding the meat and potatoes beneath the lettuce on her plate; the daughter, turning back at the threshold to her new development, crawling into bed in the middle of the day, cramming her mouth with chocolates and conjuring up the image of a mother whose life she cannot allow herself to transcend.

II

IN AN AUTOBIOGRAPHICAL BOOK published last year, I described four generations of women in my mother's family. I wrote the book because I wanted to understand the legacy of mother/daughter relationships that was my own troubled inheritance. But I had not yet understood exactly how the historic period in which my mother and I, respectively, came of age inclined one of us to develop an eating disorder while the other was relatively free of this disturbance. Now, however, it seems to me that my mother and I are a paradigm of that mother/daughter drama secretly playing out all around us. And this is true although my mother had a career and was already, early in this century, actively involved in the world. This is my mother's story.

Arriving in this country as a girl of twelve, my mother managed to learn English and graduate from primary school, to find herself faced with the necessity of working fourteen hours a day in a factory to help support the family. Later, when her father abandoned them, she became the principal wage-earner and was able to return to school only when the need for factory workers during the First World War made possible the half-day program, in which high school students could attend school until noon and then work another shift in the ammunition factory. At eighteen, my mother graduated from high school and went to New York, where she became an organizer for the Communist Party.

But my mother's life continued to be dominated by a brooding, half-conscious preoccupation with the immigrant mother she left at home, a woman victimized by a brutal husband, by neighbors who did not welcome her in this country, by the poverty that afflicted most immigrant families of her generation, and by her own troubled inability to adjust to life in the new world. Frequently, when I was a child, my mother told me about the way she had seen her mother being beaten by her father when she was too young to do anything about it. I remember the look on her face as she spoke about the time she was no longer too young. For the day finally came when my mother, still a girl, lifted a fist against her own father and said: "Never, never lay a hand on my mother or I will take a knife to you."

My grandfather did not ever lift his hand against his wife in the presence of my mother—not ever again.

I have come to think of that scene as a crucial developmental moment, a turning point in which everything my mother was to become already was present. If she now goes out into her own life to fight against patriarchal authority (which she called Capitalism and the bosses), she will do it with the knowledge that as a girl she could already stand up to her father and in the name of her mother make him back down. She had seen fear in her father's eyes. In that moment she realized that she had power.

This fight against tyrannical authority became the dominant pattern of my mother's life. For the next sixty years, as a radical organizer, she fought for the suffering, the poor, the oppressed, the broken, the humiliated, the immigrant. For she was fighting always in the name of her mother, a broken immigrant woman. In this sense the people had become her mother.

Because my mother was able to find a socially meaningful way to live out this preoccupation with her mother's life, she did not develop an eating disorder. But I did. And I developed it in fact at the age of seventeen, when I was about to enter college and thereby take my life into a sphere of development for which my own mother longed and which she had renounced. The fact that she had a career was not in itself sufficient to keep me from worrying and brooding about her. A debilitating guilt came into my life at the moment I was about to do something that she had yearned for and had failed to achieve. I was facing the daughter's problem of surpassing the mother.

In many ways, indeed, my mother's existence fulfilled that larger destiny for which women yearn. She left home at a young age, entered the radical movement in New York, and spent the next sixty.years in an intensely meaningful struggle on behalf of the working class. But I, her daughter, always sensed her unfulfilled yearning for that life of scholarship and contemplation I was myself considering when I graduated from high school. Already, at the age of seventeen, wandering around in Berlin, during months I should have been enrolled as a freshman at the University of California, I knew that I longed to become a poet and writer, that I wanted to study literature, that I felt impelled to turn away from the world of social commitment and political involvement that had been so important to my mother. Although she had raised me to become an independent woman, with the right to higher education, I sensed, also, that my mother would not feel at ease with a daughter who was shortly to become that introspective, ivory-tower intellectual I would remain for the next twenty years (until feminism taught me how I might finally reconcile my literary leanings with the political orientations of my childhood).

None of this was conscious. But in retrospect I am aware that these preoccupations with my mother's life—the contrast between her sense of intellectual inadequacy and my audacious plans to become a poet—influenced me profoundly as I walked about in Berlin wearing a cotton jacket and summer shoes, shivering in the cold, living in a worker's flat, as week after week I postponed my movement forward into that next step of development I was afraid to make. For even in those days, as I went rushing about eating chocolates and hot dogs and loaves of hot bread, at the back of my thoughts was a sustained preoccupation. Brooding there with a tremendous power, although I was only half aware of it, was an idea that emerged fleetingly into consciousness during that anguished racing to the next bakery, the next chocolate shop. It rose up and was stuffed back down with the next bite of hot black bread. But I can recall it still, some twenty-five years later, and today can make sense of the fact that my problem with food and my preoccupation with my mother came together that winter in Berlin.

For what was it I remembered about my mother's life—its heroism, its struggle, its many fulfillments? These were there, but what I remembered was the fact that at my age she had dropped out of Hunter College and always, since then, had felt intellectually inadequate and extremely ambivalent about her capacity to absorb and understand culture, which she loved.

This preoccupation with surpassing the mother is apparent in women whose development hesitates or altogether ceases as they become obsessed with food. And yet it is never easy to approach this issue. As we move toward it the conversation slows down and is filled with movements of resistance and retreat; women frequently turn in their chair or avert their face from me. Many cover their face with their hands. In the beginning, their crying remains silent. And then, suddenly, the breaking through of this old, deep preoccupation, the terrible sobbing, the wringing of hands. For who can bear this vision of the mother's life, impoverished, sacrificed, depleted?

It is perhaps the most bitter tragedy of this situation that in a crisis of development of this kind, when a woman feels unable to move out into her own life, she would wish naturally to turn to an older woman for help and support. If her mother had passed knowingly through a similar time of urgency and had been able to evolve beyond it, she could offer to her child counsel and vision, a serene knowledge that there is resolution ahead, value in crisis and struggle. Both her silent example and her active advice would be able to sustain and support her child. But when the failures of the mother's life are a vital part of the daughter's crisis, the child will feel lonely and abandoned before the immensity of this developmental task.

Very likely, if her mother has not passed through a similar stage of development but has retreated from it into the apparent safety of home and motherhood, the daughter will not even be able to recognize her dilemma as a typical crisis in development through which a later generation must be able to surpass the values and choices an earlier generation has made.

Men may take for granted the turmoil of this imperative developmental task, this necessity to face the father at the crossroads and symbolically to kill him and take his place in the world. Thus, Frederick V. Grunfeld, writing about Jewish sons at the turn of the century:

> *In accordance with the unwritten rule that sons should,*
> *wherever practicable, surpass their fathers—hence the*
> *constant, restless need to be doing something—the shoe-*
> *factory generation regularly produced and nurtured a brood of*
> *scribes, artists, intellectuals. . . . Carl Sternheim [was] the*
> *son of a banker and newspaper publisher, Walter Benjamin*
> *of an antique dealer, Alfred Neumann of a textile*
> *manufacturer, Franz Kafka of a haberdashery wholesaler,*
> *Hermann Broch of a cotton-mill owner; Theodor Lessing and*
> *Walter Hasenclever were sons of doctors and grandsons of*
> *manufacturers, and so on, in an orderly and predictable*

procession from the department store into the library, the
theatre and the concert hall.

Often this pattern involved the sons in a double revolt—
against the father's Jewish-bourgeois values, and against the
system of obedience training of German society as a whole
. . . the basic pattern, at any rate, applied to nearly all the
intellectuals; indeed, it was so pervasive that an
anthropologist might be tempted to describe them as a . . .
specialized caste of communicators and problem-solvers who
are, as it were, born to be articulate.

It is this oedipal drama, informed by childhood sexual fantasy and rivalry with the father, that Freud has placed at the
very origin of human personality. To move out successfully
into his own life, a man must be able to surmount the guilts and
imagined violences of oedipal fantasy and transform them into
a sublimated rivalry for creative stature and social place. In the
generation of German-Jewish fathers and sons Grunfeld is describing, the rivalry with the father, the sense of being called to
surpass him, actually serves as inspirational force for the son.

But for a girl in a developmental crisis this ancient myth of
Laius and Oedipus meeting for bloody confrontation at the
crossroads will not serve—unless she casts her development in
masculine terms and plays it out exclusively with respect to the
father. And here of course is yet another reason a woman seeking her own development might be inclined to take on male attire. For this act of symbolic gender transformation allows us
simultaneously to free ourselves from our mothers and to become instead our father's sons. As a woman hoping to develop
in uniquely female ways, she would have virtually no mythic
guides to elaborate the issues facing her at each stage of her development, no analysis to help her work out the strategy for resolution of her plight with reference to her mother. Nowhere

have we formulated that "unwritten rule" that girls must, wherever practicable, surpass their mothers. For female development, in this respect, we have formulated virtually nothing at all.

A daughter is unable to place her filial rivalry and conflict within the shared social expectation that she will inevitably feel this way. She is unable to appease guilt with worldly-wise reflection, to lift her eyebrows and nod her head that so must it be: one generation must proceed inexorably beyond the next. Feeling lost and helpless, confused, scarcely able to bring her distress to articulate awareness, not knowing where to turn and with whom to speak, she not surprisingly longs to clothe herself in the garments of those for whom the struggle to separate from a parent is considered necessary and essential. But it is no wonder that this strategy inevitably fails. The body gains back the weight natural to it, returns to being female, and the new clothes no longer fit. ("It is always the pants that go first. To begin with the thighs don't fit into them anymore. And then of course there's the hips. Sometimes I have the impression that the minute I look at a plate of noodles I gain ten pounds and turn into my mother.") The disguise breaks down, and with it the illusion that we can solve the problem of female identity by looking and behaving as if we were men. That anguish in front of the mirror when we are trying on a pair of pants that no longer fit is the anguish of a person confronted by the fact of being fundamentally and irrevocably female—and thereby excluded from the fully legitimate right to evolve.

Whether we experience this anguish as a fear of becoming the mother or of being doomed as her daughter to inherit her fate, the crisis is formidable and cannot be slighted even when it comes to expression as a despair about the size of hips and thighs and the cut of our clothes. Because the crisis remains opaque, leads to no further understanding of our plight, torments us with its apparent absurdity—all this grief, this anguish, this tearing of hair, this loathing for the body five or ten pounds heavier now—we are likely to reach out for some kind of immediate gratification and relief. Often the woman takes herself to bed, pulls up the covers, and tries to hide from the nameless urgency with which she suffers. And often, too, she reaches for food. This is the most bitter irony of her situation, the implicit, tragic irony in every eating disorder. Because her mother cannot give her what she needs—cannot enter with full understanding into her struggle, cannot model for her its potential resolution—she reaches for food in place of the mother and thereby incurs the terrible danger of becoming everything she most fears to be: a human being for whom the question of rightful development has not yet been formulated.

"You know what will happen to you little girl? You'll get fatter and fatter. Until your body bloats out . . . like your mother."

"What was your mother doing when she was your age?" I ask women who suffer in their relation to food. The women always know. This unexpected question leads them, after a brief hesitation in which they seem confused and troubled by this thought, to describe their mothers' lives in amazing detail, as if they have been listening with a taut, strained concentration to all her stories and secretly, unknown even to themselves, have been measuring their own lives against their mothers'.

In the lives of most men nothing suggests the need to stay closely identified with their mothers, to feel her suffering as their own, to carry the burden of her sorrow and failure. A man is expected to separate from his mother early, to know himself as other than she, to leave her behind in childhood, to follow in the footsteps of his father, to welcome her sacrifice of herself as part of what it means to be a mother. A man has little reason to brood about his mother's life at each turning and developmental passage in his own life. Whatever else he may or may not become, no matter how long and splendidly he may live, he knows from an early age that he will not become a mother.

This freedom to leave the mother behind without a debilitating concern for her is startlingly evident in Russell Baker's autobiography, *Growing Up*. In a highly instructive passage Baker describes the way, little by little, his high school education had been taking him beyond his mother's intellectual and scholastic achievements. First, he outdistances her in Latin, then in mathematics, and in so doing breaks "one of the oldest links in the chain binding [them] together." For his mother, who had been a schoolteacher, had long tutored and coached and encouraged him so that he could rise beyond the working-class conditions of his background and "make something of himself." His growth beyond her is thus, in every way, much more than an intellectual feat; it represents a developmental turning point, a movement into autonomous identity, a separation from the mother. And it involves an act of conspicuously surpassing her. This is the way he experiences it: "As my intellectual pride increased I began to take pleasure in the feeling that my education was superior to hers. For years I had heard about her year of college, her Latin classes, her schoolteacher's art, and now I was pleased to realize that despite all that, she could no longer keep up with me. One evening I yielded to an evil impulse to show her how little Latin she knew."

He tricks his mother into attempting the translation of a difficult passage he had worked out with his teacher earlier in the day. As always, she comes over to help him at his work and finds that this time she cannot translate the passage he has set before her. He then produces his correct translation and puts her to shame. Knowing what has happened, she gets up and leaves the table. "Something else that had bound us together parted that night," he writes. "It had been cruelly done, but I had issued my first declaration of independence from child-hood."

It is impossible to imagine a girl staging this little drama of mother-testing as part of her declaration of independence from childhood. It is impossible to imagine a girl serenely taking pleasure in an education superior to her mother's. If the girl child had come home from school with a task she knew was beyond her mother's ability we can imagine that she would have been keeping an anxious eye upon her mother, terrified that the older woman would, as usual, come over to offer her help. Perhaps to avoid this confrontation the daughter would have begun to feel restless at dinner, complaining of headaches, going early to bed without eating to do her schoolwork behind the closed door to her room. And maybe, even, if it grew bad enough—if this sense of what it might mean to her mother to discover that her own education, her proud years of teaching, had already been surpassed by this young girl—maybe then the daughter might even begin to do less well at Latin, to falter and begin to fail, so that she need not come square up against this confrontation with the mother that would inevitably shame the older woman and consign her to a life made even smaller by the shrinking of her nostalgic pride.

Is it a wonder, then, that so many women are tempted to take on lean, male bodies in the hope that they might escape from the mother's destiny without enduring all that remorse of leaving the mother behind? As we face the issue of surpassing the mother, how much we must yearn to be as offhand about it, as serenely cruel and self-referring as the son.

A girl must brood upon her mother's life. Everything she comes to think about the mother and the act of mothering, everything she knows and senses about the institution of mothering and the particular experience of it her own mother has known bears an immediate and urgent relevance to herself.

We know as yet very little about the 8 percent of anorexics who are male. It is possible that they are men who carry a close identification with their mother, a tendency to fret and concern themselves with their mother's life and to express their imperfect separation from their mother in the way they behave with food. But these characteristics are certainly not typical of most men, whose symbolic relation to the mother is more likely (as Freud has shown) to be mediated through the vicissitudes of their sexuality and to be built rather upon a sense of otherness than on a feeling of identification.

Recently, several therapists have told me they see a number of men who are preoccupied with food and weight and eating. This does not surprise me. It may be understood as part of the contemporary male effort to reclaim and develop in themselves qualities of feeling, sensitivity, and tenderness they have been taught to associate with women. Thus, the problem of identification and separation from the mother would indeed be brought urgently into their lives and might well lead to a preoccupation with food and weight.

There is of course a fascinating paradox in this situation, the women of our time trying to shape masculine bodies for themselves and to clothe themselves in male attire and to identify themselves with the son during the same generation when men are contemplating their identification with the mother. A man preoccupied with gaining weight, growing a belly, softening his armored musculature may well fear that he is succeeding all too well in this process of softening and opening that he associates with women and that would compel him to take on the great burden of the mother's life and destiny the daughter inevitably receives.

The contrast for most women between their life of possibility and their mother's life of limitations continues to haunt them through every stage of growth and development, making separation a perilous matter, for it involves inevitably this problem of surpassing a woman who must, in her lonely sense of failure at life, perceive the daughter's movement into the world as a betrayal and abandonment of the identity they share.

And so the mother rises up to preside over the bingeing and vomiting that offer her daughter a mute, unconscious means to express her crisis in development. She is the mother without ambition hidden away in the home. She is the working mother struggling to support her family, who sacrificed higher education for their sake. She is the responsible corporate executive, who secretly yearns for a life of freedom and irresponsibility. Or she is the mother whose body and life seem "a blob, an unformed mass, amorphous, sprawling," the description of the mother's body serving always to represent what was glimpsed and fathomed about those same unformed, undeveloped qualities in the mother's life.

In women who express their developmental crises through eating disorders, preoccupation with the mother's life frequently reaches back to inform their earliest memories, their first conscious moments of awareness of the world. I have listened to hours of intimate confession during which women struggle to bring forth memories from this earliest stratum of their imagination. I have seen their face change from a strained mask of smiling cheerfulness with which bulimic women frequently present themselves to the world. I have watched the crumbling of resistance as tears come and that other, hidden face of sorrow emerges, deepening the lines between their eyes, transforming them visibly into that anxious, watchful person they must have been as children, keeping a precocious eye on a mother who, in spite of all attempts at denial, impressed them deeply with the emptiness and impoverishment of her life.

III

WOMEN COMING OF AGE today are faced with a unique psychological task, one far different from that which confronted most women in earlier generations. When we recall Anne Hutchinson and her struggle to preach in Puritan America or remember the lonely travels of Susan B. Anthony or the courage of Sojourner Truth, who reminded a mocking world that women's lives are by their very nature filled with work and that struggle which makes our power, we are calling up foremothers who battled against a complete refusal to regard us, the world's women, as fully human beings. In those earlier generations the women who carried our struggle into the world did so not only in the name of the suffering millions of their own generations but in the name of their oppressed and humiliated mothers as well. One can easily imagine how, for them, it was precisely the haunting image of their mothers' lives that inspired them when they stepped forward, the first women to speak before legislative bodies, the first to enter the halls of higher education, the first to urge women to vote. With every step they took they could feel that the lives of women in all earlier generations moved forward with them, for they were battling the contempt and prejudices of thousands of years.

Women today have a struggle, of course; they face still the battle for child care, for an amendment that guarantees our equal rights, for our freedom to choose the time when we would give birth to our children, for equal pay, for sexual liberation, and against that racism which always implicitly includes women in its stereotypes. But for young women leaving home and entering the world today there is a new ease, a luxury that at first sight we would not take to be the cause of their troubles. I am speaking here of that luxury of a generation that did not have to struggle for the advantages that have come to it. I am thinking about the paradox of feeling that we have the right to the social advantages made available to us now while at the same time there rises within us a profound feeling of guilt as we step forward into all those opportunities our own mothers were unable to choose. This is the paradox out of which eating disorders arise, to bring growth and development to an end— thereby helping the daughter evade the problem of surpassing the mother. Because she is no longer fighting in the name of all women, the woman of today who responds to new social opportunities cannot seek from within herself the sustaining sense that what she does with her life, as a woman, will implicitly and symbolically benefit her mother. The battle today is less pitched, less militant, less tangible. And so the uneasiness rises, and faces us with a grim contradiction. To the degree that she can take her education, her profession, her social ease for granted, precisely to that degree will a woman be stricken with a form of survivor guilt.

Anorectic women are frequently described by their parents and siblings in terms that explicitly evoke the concentration camp experience. "She looks like those pictures of people just liberated from Buchenwald," a mother says to me on the telephone, describing her twenty-year-old daughter who has just dropped out of school. "I can't bear to look at her," another woman says of her younger sister. "She looks like a death's-head, like one of those people the Nazis tried to starve to death." "You go over to the high school today," says one mother of a teenage daughter to another in Aimee Liu's book, *Solitaire,* "and it's like walking into a concentration camp."

It is through pictures of starving men and women and children, newly released from concentration camps by the Allies, that most of us first came to learn of the full horror of those camps. We became familiar with the protruding bones, the sunken faces, the enormous eyes and distended bellies that mean starvation, whether imposed or self-afflicted. Although anorectic women refuse to acknowledge the extent of the physical depletion they have taken upon themselves, it is surely of interest that they have afflicted themselves with the most tragic and dramatic imagery for human devastation our culture knows. It is as if they are trying to tell us, through this imagery of their own emaciation, exactly what kind of guilt it is they are suffering from on behalf of their mother, whose life they see through this same imagery of devastation.

In reality, of course, one cannot compare the lives of privileged women of the last decades and the suffering of those who went through the horrors of the concentration camps. But symbolically it is possible for daughters to see their mother's life in these extreme terms and then to adopt, as a symbolic method of talking about this devastation, the physical imagery with which the culture is most familiar.

"After her divorce my mother could not get out of bed until late in the afternoon. I remember that. I was four years old. But already I knew how to get up and get myself dressed and make toast for myself. We lived around the corner from the school. I used to walk there alone, wearing the same dress I wore the day before. The kids used to make fun of me. In that time, when I was growing up, the girls all wore those little starched dresses, a different one every day. I had on the same graying pair of socks. We weren't poor, or anything. It was just that my mother couldn't take care of me. I made my own lunch with anything we happened to have around the house. All the other kids had these little sandwiches carefully cut. I remember that. The mothers in that time were always trying to come up with something special. But mine was still in bed when I got home from school. And then, when she finally dragged herself out, I'll never forget it. That look on her face. It was . . . I can't bear to remember.'' She covers her face with her hands. ''I can see it still, but I don't want to see it.'' She presses her fists into her eyes. ''No, go away,'' she cries out. ''She looked like death. Like the face of death itself. Gray, withered.''

The mothers of anorexics describe their daughters as concentration camp victims; the daughters see death in their mothers' faces. At the moment the girl needs to separate from the older woman, and leave her behind, we find her taking on a gray, pale cast, her body losing flesh as if she were aging. She is withering when she could be blossoming. In the full flush of youth she is becoming middle-aged. She has made herself over into an exaggerated reflecting mirror in which we behold all those qualities of devastation that are sometimes implicit, sometimes evident in her mother's life.

Women who suffer from bulimia do not always bring about a state of emaciation that reflects the most poignant form of mass suffering our culture has known. But they, too, feel a deep guilt about their mothers and describe their lives with a characteristic type of imagery. The vocabulary of women who suffer from eating disorders is filled with words like *shrunken, impoverished, exhausted, drained, depleted, all used up, stripped, sucked dry, totally empty, all spread out.* Often, this suggestive imagery is used to describe the woman's mother. Often it describes what their own lives have become since they developed an eating problem.

''My mother's life? You want me to talk about my mother's life? It's a disaster area. When I go to visit her it feels to me as if

I'm walking into a bomb shelter. You know? Where the bomb already fell? It's a wasteland. A camp for displaced persons. You get the point? My mother's a victim. A sacrificial victim.''

Would we expect a woman who feels like this to skip out happily into those new opportunities made available in this generation? Would we expect her to open the metaphoric door to her own life and blithely slam behind her that literal door that shuts her mother into domesticity and depletion? No one expects the survivor of a holocaust to enter easily into life when friends and family have been destroyed. We may resist the comparison. But women suffering from eating disorders are trying to tell us that their mothers' lives have impressed them through their suffering and devastation.

For this particular daughter, who sees her mother as a sacrificial victim, entry into her mother's life is always disturbing. And it always calls up a problem with food. She describes her mother's house: a place ''where the television is always on. The house is perfectly neat. My mother is well off, she doesn't have to worry about money. But there's something in the way she sits there, her hands folded in her lap, her lips pressed together . . . I bring her books, she thumbs through them and puts them aside. She's an educated woman but I think she's practically forgotten how to read. She gave everything for the family. And then, when I, the youngest, left home, my father abandoned her and her life just died.''

This daughter, who lives three thousand miles away from her mother, comes home four times a year to visit. Each time, although she has not suffered from bulimia for several years, she finds herself rushing into the kitchen to eat ''all the junk food in sight'' whenever her mother gets on the phone. Then she goes into the toilet to vomit.

''As if you're vomiting up your mother's life?''

She puts her hand over her mouth. "Oh, God," she says. "That's it, isn't it? I'm vomiting up my mother's life."

Actual concentration camp survivors, often for many years after their release, continue to dwell upon moments when against all odds they might have turned back to help a mother or father, shared some last crust of bread, or given up a ragged piece of blanket. And so, too, women with eating disorders dwell on their past, recalling their childhood in a way that suggests they blame themselves for the suffering of their mother.

For this reason a feminist analysis is frequently so liberating for these daughters, who otherwise fail to see themselves as part of a generation struggling for development their own mothers lacked. They can describe with heartbreaking precision all the sufferings their mother endured, broken dreams, failed promises, the hardship and sacrifices of raising children, but it rarely occurs to them that their mother shared this fate with most of the other women of her time. Instead, they tend to explain their mother's life as if they themselves, from earliest infancy, drained and depleted the mother with the intensity of their needs.

"She was totally different before she got married and had children. You should see her wedding picture. You should see pictures of her when she was engaged to my father. I have one picture of my mother skiing. She was so full of life, so full of hope, she stood there with her shoulders back, her head lifted. She looks like a woman who could go out and conquer the world."

"And then what happened to her?"

"I was born. And then my sister. We did it. I was the oldest and I probably did it most of all. She wasn't familiar with being a mother. She worried a lot. I was a difficult child, she always told me that. I woke up at night, I exhausted her. She never recovered."

Daughters and Mothers

In the private mythology of the daughter, it is not circumstance, domestic ideology, the failure of dreams and ambition that have harmed the mother; it is the daughter, who blames herself and carries a remorseless guilt. Not surprising, then, that she pauses at the call to her own liberation and turns back, brooding over her mother's life.

" 'Abandon hope, all ye who enter here': that's what someone ought to pin up over the door of my mother's house." The woman speaking, with a suppressed bitterness, these words Dante placed over the entrance to hell was once a graduate student in comparative literature. Several years ago she dropped out of school in order, as she says, "to devote myself more completely to my obsession with food."

"But you haven't in fact given up all hope."

"I haven't?"

"Don't you call her every time you're in trouble?"

"I ask her to send money—that at least she can do. Financially, she can always support me."

"And so you are letting her give to you in the only way she can?"

This comment stops, for a long time, any further conversation. She closes her eyes, she leans forward over her knees. Several times I have the impression she is about to begin talking and then stops herself. And suddenly, in a great rush of words, she says:

"Are you suggesting I have this food thing, this breakdown because I wanted to give my mother the chance to mother me? In the only way she's ever likely to be able? Are you saying that's why I can't become independent? Because I need to give her this . . . gift of my life? Is that it? I'm sacrificing myself to my mother . . . by falling apart? I develop an eating problem. I refuse to eat. In a sense, then, she has to feed me?"

The daughter blames herself for the mother's sacrifice, feels an overweening guilt, and becomes then in her own right a sacrifice to the mother. Beneath the diversity of their symptoms, women troubled in their relation to food tend to have certain conspicuous traits in common. Whether they suffer from compulsive eating or bulimia or anorexia; whether they seek ardently for control or experience episodes of bacchanalian release; whether they hoard food for secret eating at night or secretly throw it away to give others the impression they have eaten, they all are deeply preoccupied with making some return to their mother for the sorrows and deprivations they believe they have caused.

They rush home to take the mother to a dental appointment. They race in to carry on negotiations between the mother and another child. They are the go-betweens carrying resolutions back and forth between embattled parents. It is difficult for them to surrender to the passions and enthusiasms of their own life, for they are busy brooding about their mother's well-being, trying to anticipate her every need and to offer "some return for everything she has given. Sure, call it reparations if you will. It's her turn now, isn't it?"

A young woman gets to her feet in amazement, her hands pressed against her temples, as she suddenly understands the significance of a memory dating back to her earliest years. "I had a little jewelry box when I was three or four years old—all sorts of silly trinkets that I loved. But my favorite treasure was a shiny new copper penny my uncle gave me. I wrapped it up in tin foil to keep it safe. But at night I used to sit on my bed and unwrap it, just to look at it shine. For me it was all the gold and jewels in the world. I loved it. But you know what I did with this penny one day after my mother and I had a fight? I took it and put it on my mother's dresser. I was maybe three or four years old at the time. And I gave her my copper penny. I gave her the very best thing I had in the world."

The woman remembering the copper penny first came to speak with me many months after she had already "conquered" her problems with anorexia. She no longer made herself fast for weeks after a large meal. She was no longer "a living skeleton." But she was still, several years after the outbreak of preoccupation with losing weight, unable to return to school. She worked for a minimal wage in a job far below her capacities. Her life bored and frustrated her. She suffered from a feeling of meaninglessness, from a sense that she was "living a death" and was still a "walking skeleton."

Her story is a particularly revealing account of the hidden drama between mother and daughter that ultimately gives rise to eating problems and continues to afflict both the older woman and her child even after the obvious symptoms of an eating obsession have vanished. I asked her permission to tell it here at length, and she hesitated for several weeks. But one day she suddenly said with great feeling: "Tell it, tell my story. Sometimes I sit in my room alone and I think, 'If only they knew. If only they understood. If only they had an idea what it was like to have a life dry up and wither on you like that. If they only knew . . .' "

The facts are straightforward: Florence was her mother's youngest daughter. She graduated with highest honors in mathematics from a prestigious Ivy League school. An older brother and sister had already graduated from college. Her mother had dropped out of law school some twenty years before.

How we interpret these facts, however, is problematic: Florence's mother, she said, had decided years before, when her older brother was born, that her legal studies were damaging to him. She had listened to her mother tell this story many times. But she did not believe her mother's repeated assurance that she never regretted the decision to sacrifice her career.

And there are, of course, certain details of which we must take particular note: when Florence grew up, graduated from college, and applied to law school, her mother also decided to resume her legal career. She says: "My mother suddenly looked ten years younger. She got herself new clothes, she lost weight, the color came back into her cheeks. She no longer looked exhausted. I went shopping with her and we bought new clothes. It was like going to school with my sister. We loved it. I was happy my mom was going to do something with her life."

Soon, indeed, as the daughter tells it, the whole family enters into this excitement. The older sister buys identical tweed jackets for the mother and the daughter. The older brother, himself a lawyer, offers a competition. He will send on vacation to Hawaii the woman who proves to be most successful at this new career. Mother and daughter will compete for highest grades, the loser to be determined by the first to receive anything less than an A.

And now the story unfolds along predictable lines. During the first semester mother and daughter both receive straight A's on their final reports. This surprises no one. They are both devoted to their studies and spend long hours in the library, sitting across from one another at the oak table. They meet in the morning for early coffee to review what they have studied the night before. The first mother and daughter enrolled together in courses, they become well known at their school. In the second semester the daughter's grades continue to be perfect, but the mother receives a B-plus in torts. In the third semester the daughter develops a serious problem with bulimic anorexia. Six weeks later she drops out of school.

At this point in the story the daughter experiences difficulty talking. She looks angry and surprised, as if she had never heard her story like this before. She stands up and paces. When she sits down she draws her chair closer to me and speaks rapidly.

A year after the daughter has dropped out of school the mother is still attending classes. The daughter, against great odds, manages then to enroll in another, even more prestigious school on the East Coast. Within several weeks, however, her anxiety proves to be overwhelming. She continues to be bothered by a growing obsession with bingeing and fasting and vomiting. She loses fifteen pounds. She again drops out of school.

By the time the mother graduates from law school the daughter weighs ninety pounds. She has by then spent two years as a secretary in a neighborhood legal advice center. She has no plans to return to law school. She claims to be very happy about her mother's career. She regrets deeply the fact that she must turn to her mother frequently for financial support.

For this daughter, the eating problem has become a way to stop her own development, to leave the field open to the mother, to withdraw from the competition between them, to sacrifice herself for the older woman's sake. But now the daughter says something she has not told me before. She remembers to stress the fact that in the first year after leaving law school she returned to live at home. Because she felt unable to support herself, because she couldn't manage her anxiety, because she was obsessed with losing weight and couldn't concentrate on even routine work, she spent her days lying in bed while she waited for her mother and father to return home. At dinner the daughter pretended to eat, cutting the food up into small pieces, slipping the meat off her plate into the mouth of the family dog. And then, because the daughter was consistently losing weight, the mother began to come home early from work and now is interrupting her career to prepare special meals for her daughter, whose appearance troubles her greatly.

"Beside herself," as the daughter says, and not knowing what else to do, the mother continually "pushes food" at her. And soon, as the daughter recalls it, all conversation in the family is about food. For this daughter has lost all other interest in life.

"I was," she says, "back in the condition of a tiny infant." And now telling me this the daughter begins to cry. "I woke, I sobbed, I waited for my mother to come. She sat on the edge of my bed. She fed me and I ate."

And so we see the way in which the daughter succeeds in returning her life to her mother. She sacrifices her own growth and development, the promise of a career, the close friendships she has formed, the lovers and admirers she has been so proud of. Returning home, she offers to the older woman that very opportunity to mother her the older woman could not take when her daughter was a child. For this is what we have come to realize as the weeks of our conversation unfold. The daughter has found missing pieces in her memory of her mother's life. Soon, she recalls how the older woman, exhausted by conflict and by the raising of two older siblings, had made upon her, from the earliest years, a devastating impression.

"She was never able to mother me," she admits one day in a tiny voice, whispering as she looks anxiously around the room, as if she were telling the most carefully guarded secret of their lives. "It was my sister who took care of me. My mother couldn't do it. I know she felt guilty about it," the daughter says. "I know it worried her. She could never forgive herself for letting me down that way. But was it her fault? They never called it a breakdown but I knew. After my birth, my mother simply wasn't the same woman anymore. Later, when I was older, I used to hear about the way she had been before I was born. But the mother I saw was always slumped over the kitchen table in a pair of old jeans. When I came in she tried to pretend she hadn't been weeping. I thought, although I didn't know it at the time . . . nevertheless I was always thinking: 'I did this to her. I did this thing.' "

Here, the conversation stops for long moments. The daughter of the woman who could not mother her sits bent over her knees. She does not want me to see that she is weeping. She has buried her head in her hands. I hear a blue jay cawing on the roof, a cat walks down the rose tree by the door outside the window. A car draws up on the street. These things become noteworthy because of this silence in which she discovers a truth.

Finally, she raises her head.

"Naturally," she says, "I gave her my copper penny. Naturally," she says, "I gave her my life."

IV

WE ARE LIVING IN a time when the institution of motherhood has broken down, although few of us who mother are able to acknowledge this. We pull ourselves together when someone walks into the room. We hurry through the house putting things in order an hour before the children come home from school. We straighten the closets, the shelves, the alcove, the attic space. And then when some trivial object gets out of place and intrudes upon the order we have imposed, something inside us seems to tear free. We turn, wild-eyed, filled with rage against the trangressor, words of abuse and reproach on our lips. We have reached a breaking point we try to hide from others and from ourselves. And meanwhile our daughters know. They know our secret. Their crisis has become public and dramatic, ours remains hidden. Their breakdown is reflecting ours.

Virtually every woman who has come to talk to me about a serious problem with eating believes that her mother experienced stress so severe in mothering her that between us we are forced to wonder whether it was a breakdown. As daughters, it is difficult for us to acknowledge this. It feels as if we are revealing the most strenuously kept secret of our childhood and family life. It feels, merely in acknowledging the fact of our mother's crisis, that we are betraying her, we who know how militantly she struggled to ward off her crisis in mothering and to keep it hidden. And yet, as the weeks and months of our work proceed, we come to see that this knowledge of trouble and disorder in our mother's life has always been there. Somehow, she managed to hide it from others. From her husband, who was too busy, too absorbed in work to notice; who took it for granted, perhaps, the inevitable strain and stress of raising children. And we, meanwhile, who suffer guilt and despair in our relation to food, have gone on hiding from ourselves the guilt and despair we feel about this secret knowledge of the trouble in our mother's life.

Let no one hear this as a blaming of the mothers. Mothers have a right to their anguish, to their conflict, to their doubt and ambivalence and uncertainty about their roles. Surely we can speak of it, analyse it, brood upon it, lament it on their behalf and on behalf of their daughters, without walking into the camp of those who blame the mothers? Or, to put this another way: why should a woman, because she gives birth to a child, cease to be troubled by profound social and cultural and existential questions? And why, if we raise these questions for her, should it be imagined that we blame her for an inability to silence them? Imagine a man ceasing to ponder the problems of culture and society, identity and value, simply because he has become a father. And yet, this expectation is what we bring to any woman who becomes a mother—imagining that somehow, through this biological act, she should be miraculously freed from the questions and problems with which her culture has faced her. To say that women of our time experience a profound, remorseless conflict about motherhood and that this uncertainty and this resentment have had an impact upon their daughters, making it difficult for the younger women to separate from them and get on with their own lives, does not commit us to the blaming of the mothers. Surely it is time to free both mother and child from the need to hide the raw anguish by which our mothers have lived? For it is this hiding and disguising, rather than the anguish itself, that is causing trouble for both mothers and daughters of this generation, whether we see ourselves as the mother or as her child.

I remember the day in my consultation room when I became aware of this dual identification. I was speaking to a young woman of twenty-two who had dropped out of school and was working as a waitress. I listened to her talk about her mother's frantic search for something meaningful, the way she was continually and urgently redecorating the house, the way she had joined and left numerous religious sects, the way she had taken up and put down various arts and handicrafts, all with a rather driven, desperate air, as if she were barely managing to keep herself together. I smiled to myself, recognizing the portrait. It could have been any of a dozen friends and acquaintances of my own. And then I stopped smiling. This woman, this mother, was my age. My daughter was the age of the young woman who had come to consult with me. It had never occurred to me before. After twenty years of being a mother I thought of myself still as a daughter struggling to separate from my mother. I had never stopped to think of myself as belonging to an entire generation of women who had raised children and for whom *we* were the mothers, those awesome and difficult and troublesome beings from whom they in turn were struggling for separation.

Many women of my age have difficulty thinking of themselves as mothers. No matter how hard we have tried, we have never succeeded wholeheartedly in embracing the maternal role. We are later in time and further along in the evolution of our desperation than were the women of whom Betty Friedan wrote, giving voice to their silenced and secret unhappiness. In talking about the women who became mothers during the

1960s and 1970s we may need to speak about their actual crisis and impending breakdown.

And so we come in this process of unraveling to a highly complex relationship between mother and child. So far we have kept our gaze primarily upon the daughters, observing the way the symptomatology of an eating disorder can be stripped back to reveal a generational breakdown within which we discover a serious identity crisis, at the heart of which there is in turn a mother/daughter separation struggle. Now I am suggesting that the daughter's breakdown mirrors a yet more hidden crisis in the mother's life, which has been concealed behind the four walls of the home and silenced by a domestic conspiracy that aims to protect the mother from exposure while in fact assigning her to a harsh and lonely suffering she is not permitted to acknowledge.

This hidden crisis in the mother, of which the daughter comes slowly and reluctantly to speak, is rarely sudden or dramatic; it takes place slowly, year after year gathering force, the despair and desperation growing steadily until they thrust themselves forth finally and make their claim upon her behavior. Frequently, the mother's crisis expresses itself in domestic terms, that failure to keep herself going at the daily routine although she continues to insist that she loves her life as a housewife and values above all else the requirements of domesticity.

For other women the crisis expresses itself in what appears to be a perfect mastery of domestic detail, within which there is in fact a rigid, life-denying insistence upon neatness and order in domestic life. The mother who insists upon baking her own bread, refuses to use paper diapers for her children, and drives herself to impossible extremes cleaning out drawers and attics and basements often seems in her daughter's eyes to be a woman at the edge, struggling against that same sense of inner chaos and near collapse far more evident in the woman who sits weeping at the table, who cannot get out of bed until noon, and whose untidy house reflects her state of inner discord.

This vision of the mother as woman at the edge is one the daughter rarely shares with anyone else, especially when her mother is a woman devoted to the supreme fulfillment of domestic norms. Her husband, friends, and acquaintances frequently admire the way she keeps such firm control over the domestic routine. They do not think of her as a woman in desperate trouble, attempting to control a sense of intense, unremitting inner conflict or impending collapse.

Her daughter, seeking help and consultation because she feels out of control of her life and desperate in her relationship to food, initially tries to present her mother as the older woman has always tried to present herself. "We had a 'casual' household," she says and means that weeks of dishes sat in the sink, the bathtub overflowed with wash, kitty litter was spilled in the hall closet, beds went unmade, and meals went uncooked as the "casual" mother appeared harried and driven. "She was an impeccable housekeeper," another daughter proudly reports. But then she remembers the look in her mother's eyes, a look of mingled wrath and desperation, and recalls the mother's sudden outburst of rage that went on and on, uncontrollable when a dish was left in the sink or when the girl's laundry was not correctly folded. She remembers the mother tight and tense, "screwed to the breaking point," sometimes yelling, sometimes freezing into silence for some petty infraction of a rule.

"I'd walk in after school and I'd have the sense I was walking into a mine field. You never knew when it would come. My mind would race. Had I made my bed properly? Had I finished the ironing? We each had our tasks. But she worked harder than any of us. Our house was spotless. There was never a dish out of place. But underneath all this order was a sense . . . how shall I call it? As if everything, at any moment, was just about to break loose and blow itself sky high . . .''

This sense of the mother's actual or impending breakdown has burdened the childhood and adolescence of women with eating disorders. Again and again we find a vision, carefully hidden, of the mother's inner collapse and emotional crisis. A clean house hiding a mine field. A neat and ordered domesticity concealing the reality of a woman too frantic to respond to the emotional stress and tension in her daughter's life. Is it possible then that our daughters break down because they have inherited a progressively growing crisis in the institution of motherhood itself?

V

WE MAY LOOK AT the twentieth century as a period in which
most of the ideas we have taken for granted where women's
lives are concerned have broken down—and above all, the concept of necessity. It is an old, hallowed idea, most often taken
for granted. In that form, as a notion of something larger than
the self, which required the subordination of the self, it was a
powerful means of accepting and ennobling conditions for women
that were at heart degrading. The feminine mystique, which
assures a woman she will be most highly satisfied by choosing
marriage and maternity, rests upon the idea that women will be
fulfilled by following their biological nature. But the feminine
mystique is a concept of personal fulfillment, not of necessity; it
is more concerned with choice and personal satisfaction, less
with the true nature of things. The idea of necessity relates the
individual life to larger entities—society, the will of God, divine
providence, natural law. It has the ring of the inevitable, the
universally binding and self-evident. "Man is born to toil,
woman is born to suffer," the members of the family say to one
another at night on the porch after the day's work, speaking as
it has been spoken for countless generations. "A man works
from sun to sun, woman's work is never done."

Where women were concerned this sense of necessity was
made up of a linked chain of diverse suppositions that were

taken for truths—that childbirth is necessarily painful; that women are necessarily less intelligent and more emotional than men; that it is necessary to have as many children as nature decrees; that women are necessarily less capable of the work of sublimation that builds culture; that it is necessarily true that childbirth and maternity call upon all of women's creative power; that it is necessary to give up one's life and dreams and desires for the good of the family; that the sacrifice and subordination of women to domesticity are necessary for the sake of the child.

Thomas Carlyle, in other respects a bold thinker, declared himself without the least self-consciousness on this issue of nature's laws, taking for granted the unquestioning agreement of his reader. "The man should bear rule in the house and not the woman. This is an eternal axiom, the law of Nature herself which no mortal departs from unpunished . . . it is the nature of a woman to cling to the man for support and direction, to comply with his humors . . . simply because they are his; to reverence while she loves him, to conquer him not by her force but her weakness."

All major political struggles by women during the twentieth century have addressed themselves to these suppositions of necessity and have, gradually, eroded them. The struggle for birth control, the discovery of anesthetics, the women's suffrage movement, the women's liberation movement, the increasing contribution of women to culture and art have begun little by little to replace these assumptions with new and radical assertions about woman's nature. But in so doing they have taken away a powerful means of suppressing and silencing discontent with the institution of maternity as it is practiced in this culture.

Although rarely discussed in these larger terms, the loss for women of this sense of necessity has been similar in its impact to the loss of belief in God. The sense of a divine, all-powerful benevolence ruling the world and rewarding goodness helped make tolerable the suffering of the innocents, the oppression of the weak, the tyrannies of the mighty, and the reign of injustice that far too frequently seems to govern human life. Once lost, however, life presents itself in its anguishing absurdity; angst that has been contained and made manageable breaks through into consciousness and dominates life. One questions the meaning and value of existence, suicide becomes a relevant alternative to the pressure and stress of living, and the modern, doubting, existential world is born.

Among women, even among those who do not think of themselves in philosophic terms, a similar process has been taking place, but far more silently and surreptitiously. Having once lost belief in the necessary sacrifice of women to marriage and maternity, most women find their domestic lives intolerable and are without means to endure their discontent in the name of something larger than themselves.

How much less painful it is to enter the limited world of marriage and domesticity if one really believes one has followed an unalterable path, walked by women generation after generation. Whatever privations and sacrifices are involved, a woman will be able to do what her mother has done, perhaps even with joy, if she sees the mother's life in terms of God-given injunctions or natural law.

The difference between women who have brought children into the world in the second half of the twentieth century and all earlier generations of women is the degree to which belief in the necessary self-sacrifice of women to domesticity has been lost. The women of the feminine mystique, whom Friedan observed, had begun to experience desperation as housewives precisely because they could no longer refer their condition to anything larger than the notion of personal fulfillment. Consequently, when the actual conditions of their lives as wives and mothers failed to meet their expectations of supreme personal satisfaction, their discontent could not be soothed by ideas of an overarching necessity weaving their individual sufferings into the grand scheme of things. They had become part of the generation of modern mothers—women who still, on the whole, tend to make this sacrifice of themselves without any longer whole-heartedly believing that it is necessary.

Naturally, there were women of this type, just as there were unbelievers, before the twentieth century. But unusually large and growing numbers of women in our time have been unable to efface themselves as human beings through the act of motherhood. They present to their daughters a fundamentally new type of mother/daughter bond, which tends to inhibit the daughter's development at that very moment when we might look forward to the daughter's liberation. For the mother of the modern day is a woman who knows that the world of larger possibilities stands open before her but has not yet been able to make the choice to enter it. Mothers and daughters of the modern era face one another, therefore, as beings in struggle for a self—the older woman having already failed in this quest as the younger starts out on it. This is the psychological background to the epidemic of eating disorders among women today.

Undoubtedly there were in earlier generations individual mothers and daughters, here and there, who struggled through the problem of female development that contemporary women face. More typical, however, were four types of mother/daughter bond around which there arose the issue of the daughter's development outside of marriage and maternity, if it arose at all. Although each of them presented mother and daughter with distinctive difficulties, each made the daughter's development possible without calling up the guilt of surpassing the mother.

It will be worth our while to look closely at these earlier

bonds. They will help us understand why the problem of transcending the conditions of one's mother's life did not arise before our time in significant numbers, bringing with it the eating obsessions that have such severely debilitating impact upon a daughter's self-development.

Through the stories of the suffragists and my own mother we have already encountered the political daughter who enters the world and fights its injustice in the name of her mother. Here, the oppression of the mother, her exclusion from culture and society, is clear and evident. The mother has not been able to struggle against it and may not consciously be aware of the need to do so. But the objective conditions of her life (the fact that she lacks the vote, is poor, has too many children, is mistreated by her husband, has no say in her own destiny) inspire the daughter to struggle on her behalf, on behalf of all women or of all oppressed people. For a daughter in this role there is no brooding uncertainty about what it will mean to the mother for the daughter to surpass the conditions of the mother's life. The daughter's struggle includes the mother within it.

Another less common type of mother/daughter bond exists when the mother and daughter both stand outside the oppressive system, united in some common effort. Here we have the daughter as co-conspirator with the mother in a situation where the mother and daughter can support and inspire one another. The Pankhursts, mother and daughters, exemplified this bond in their struggle for the vote for women in England. There can be problems for the daughter here. She may disagree with her mother and wish to go her own way within their common cause. But in general the daughter's development can be actively supported by the mother, who stands to gain a compatriot and comrade.

Earlier generations were familiar with the mother who strongly identified with her class or her position as a domesticated woman—that mother who could serve as a clear, strong opposition to the daughter's yearning to move beyond the conditions in which the older woman had lived. Here the mother exhibits no pronounced yearning to live on the wild side, to liberate her sensuality or her artistic gift or to struggle for the rights of an oppressed class. She lives surrounded by the support of domestic ideology, by the power of class identity, and by the generations of women who have chosen as she has. The daughter is free to rebel, to take her own path, to go her own way, without worrying about the devastating impact this choice might have on the mother. Jessica Mitford describes a daughter of this type in her autobiographical book, *Daughters and Rebels*. She came from the upper class, involved herself in radical, left-wing politics, moved to America, and spent her life in the radical movement. She is not the daughter fighting on behalf of the mother, but the daughter as rebel fighting against the values by which the mother lives. Here, too, the problem of surpassing the mother is not felt, since the mother is perceived to be strong and powerful in her own right, representative of women's conventional destiny and supported in this stance by the common approbation of the world. The daughter rebelling against the mother in this way would have to be less concerned with surpassing, more concerned with measuring up to her mother and acquiring the stature the mother is accorded. She is in danger of arousing her mother's anger, but not the more troublesome, more hidden emotion of resentment. She need not fear the mother's envy, for the mother experiences no seething, suppressed, ambiguous yearning for a life she cannot permit herself to have.

And then, finally, we come to the most common type of earlier mother/daughter bond. I speak here of the mother who is still able to live vicariously through her child, actively supporting the daughter's development because she sees it as part of her own, as her opportunity to do with her life what she has not yet done. To become a mother of this type a woman must have been able to reconcile herself to the idea of sacrificing herself for her child. If she can do this she will be able to support her daughter's development because she feels that the daughter will be in a position to make some return to the mother for what she has been given. Problems may arise for the daughter if she chooses to live out her own dreams and finds that these are not what the mother wishes. But if she is able to fulfill the mother's yearning she will not, as a daughter, need to be concerned about the mother's failure in life because she is actively carrying the mother's ambition out into the world so that the older woman may live vicariously through her.

There are, of course, other possibilities of bonding between mother and child. There is the weak, dependent, unhappy mother who needs to keep her daughter so closely tied to her that no separation or development is possible at all, and the mother so full and complete in herself she can encourage the daughter's development even when she cannot join it or live vicariously through it. No doubt most mothers and daughters of earlier generations fell between these two extremes. But the issue of a mother as a woman with her own highly individual and ambivalent yearnings for a destiny and self-fulfillment that she could not ask her daughter to fulfill for her had not yet commonly entered culture.

And so we come, once again, to explore in detail the way our lives as contemporary women have made the issue of development uniquely problematic for our daughters. The political daughter, the rebel, the co-conspirator, the daughter of the dream—any one of these possibilities would allow a daughter to seek her own development without dreading its impact upon her mother. What is it about us as mothers and daughters that makes these patterns so unlikely to occur in those hundreds of thousands of families where daughters develop eating disorders?

Clearly, a daughter cannot fight in the name of her mother's oppression if the mother needs to insist and requires the daughter to believe that no oppression exists. This ambiguity about the real condition of the mother will be particularly difficult to clarify when the quality of oppression is less a question of poverty, disenfranchisement, or subjection to a tyrannical husband and more a question of the meaning and value in a life. Daughters today, turning back to brood upon their mother's life, must necessarily feel deeply confused about whether the older woman is indeed suffering in the way they sense. And so we find them, mother and daughter, both cast off into that infinite loneliness of pretense and disguise, each hiding from the other the truth of the older woman's life, the daughter caught between her own and her mother's denial of the older woman's plight. No, this is not a condition under which daughters can rush out to battle oppression in their mother's name.

But, likewise, few women alive today have mothers who clearly and unambiguously stand for the traditional role of women; few have experienced their mothers as women who could easily identify themselves with generations of forebears they revere and seek to emulate and whose values and ideals they wish to hand down to their daughters. Daughters who sense the struggle and severe ambivalence in their mothers do not easily become rebels, for they know that any direct, overt opposition to the older woman is likely to tip the balance and plunge her over into that inner chaos and uncertainty she has so poignantly been trying to control.

A mother with an unfulfilled yearning for her own destiny—who has been unable either to search it out or to wholeheartedly sacrifice it for her daughter—is not a woman who will be able to enter vicariously into the life of her child, for she is a person whose trouble with maternity means, among other things, that she can no longer live through another person. She has too much sense of self, too much need for fulfillment in other terms, too much knowledge of the possibilities of such fulfillment, for that, after all, is what her ambivalence as a mother is all about. She is, moreover, a woman who does not feel she has a right to the vicarious identification that might relieve her bitter sense of unfulfillment and impoverishment. For at heart she knows herself to be a person who could never fully embrace the sacrifice of self to child.

And so this mother of the modern day, with her emerging, frustrated, ambivalent sense of self and her silenced sense of failure, cannot become her daughter's co-conspirator and join forces with her against a tyrannical, patriarchal system that has done so little to articulate or to solve the dilemma of the mother-as-woman, a person with an imperative need for life and development beyond marriage and maternity. To become her daughter's co-conspirator she would have to admit her conflict and ambivalence, acknowledge the nearness or actuality of breakdown, become fully conscious of her discontent, the hushed, unspoken sense of her life's failure. She would need to reach back for that moment in her life when she too struggled with these issues and turned around to brood about her mother's life. She would need a great deal of political knowledge and a vast amount of courage and no small store of cunning, and above all she would need permission to tell the truth about her envy and resentment of her daughter.

VI

WE HAVE ARRIVED AT the underside of the mother/daughter
bond, the unsweetened bitterness of it. To envy one's child, to
want what she has, to feel that her having it has been at one's
own expense—what a cruel and terrible irony it is to envy her
the very opportunities one longed so urgently to give her.

As a mother, I came to an understanding of these women
through my own introspection. And therefore I have allowed
myself to observe something even more difficult to acknowledge than the secret crisis of the mother's life. For the type of
mother/daughter relationship most commonly brought into my
consultation room is one in which the mother felt a keen and
exasperating envy of the daughter's opportunity, a resentment
of the relative ease with which she seemed able to go off into this
new world of opportunity opening around her before her eating
problem developed and brought this movement to an end.

A mother's envy of a beloved child. As a mother there are
few emotions more difficult to ponder. Naturally, we want the
best for our daughters, everything we were ourselves denied,
and to this end we sacrifice ourselves unstintingly. What, then,
do we make of this exasperation we feel as we listen to them talk
about the "new woman"? What, then, shall we say about this
rancor rising in us, sometimes undeniably, when we overhear
them gossiping about the future, planning to have three chil-

dren and travel all over the world and become a painter and
make a fortune on the stock market besides? And do we have to
suppress a bitter laugh, a knowing sigh, a shake of the head that
says of course we've heard it all before? A mother's envy.

Typically, the mother of the women who came to speak with
me had known the possibilities of choice in her own life. She
had received education, often higher education, and had frequently begun a career. She had chosen to renounce these as
part of the self-sacrifice that seems to go along with mothering
but was never able fully to embrace the sacrifice. She felt envy
of her daughter, and she felt resentment.

This anger about sacrificing oneself for one's child is apparent also in women who attempt to combine career or vocation
with maternity. Then, of course, the question becomes a matter of daily, repeated choices that call up uncertainty and anguish and rage. Whether to let the child watch television so that
one can draw or paint. Whether to serve frozen spinach because it will not require washing and will therefore leave one
free for that extra ten minutes of contemplation and absorp-
tion. Whether to leave her an hour or two longer at the
kindergarten so that one can take a class. Sometimes one decides it one way, sometimes the other. One starts to meditate
but then jumps to one's feet and rushes off late to pick up the
child right after school, after all.

As daughters, we always knew about our mother's resentment, however heriocally the older woman tried to disguise her
trouble. And yet, for the mother's sake, the daughter doesn't
want to know. She saw that her mother kept trying and failing;
she heard her insist that it was woman's highest good to make
sacrifices for her family. She listened to her deny in the next
breath that what she was doing was a sacrifice. She saw her
spend an entire day baking sourdough Swedish rye of the sort
her grandmother used to bake. She felt the urgency with which

the older woman looked around the table, watching her children's faces, trying to justify through their responses the day's expenditure of energy. She noticed the way the bowls of yeast and flour sat in the sink for a long time after that day, as if her mother could not bring herself to wash them out and put them away. It was the eldest daughter who washed them out and put them away, the same woman who a few years later began to starve herself. For she knew that the battle with the bread rising, on top of everything else, had enraged her mother.

She watched her mother go back and forth in the grocery store between the frozen food section and the fresh vegetables. She saw her pick up a package of frozen spinach, smiling with a strained expression as she told the daughter, who was still only a child, that this time it would be all right, did it matter if they had frozen food this one time for dinner? The daughter watched her suddenly turn and rush back over to the frozen foods and put the spinach away as if it were a filthy object. She followed her over to the vegetable counter, saw her mother pick up the fresh spinach and look tired suddenly, and sullen, and glance at her watch and put the spinach in the basket and then put it back on the counter. She went trooping behind her mother to the frozen foods, where again the mother picked up the package of frozen spinach and turned, says her daughter, with a "wild and hunted look." And so it went, back and forth, both of them trying to laugh at it, trying to pretend it was a game, this anguished journey from maternal obligation to free choice, through which the older woman was expressing her uncertainty and resentment about her role. The daughter remembers. How her mother finally brought home the fresh spinach, which wilted in the refrigerator and was never cooked. She remembers knowing about her mother's anger from the way food was bought and stored and prepared.

As an adult, the daughter interprets. She says that her

mother could no longer accept the limitations of her life. She acknowledges that her mother resented motherhood bitterly, often sabotaged it, felt envy of the daughter for being able to make other choices, was often competitive with her, and was in the end always defeated by her own ambivalence. And because the older woman was so deeply ashamed of these feelings, she often did not know she felt them at all, although the daughter sensed them.

Daughters raised in an atmosphere of mystification and ambivalence of this sort will inevitably be troubled as they go off into their own lives. They will be faced with a terrible inner division as they try to assure themselves that their mother was happy with the sacrifices she made for her daughter's sake, while at the same time they are telling themselves there was no sacrifice. Desperately, the daughter tries to banish her own anger and sense of emotional deprivation as she assures herself that there was no reason to feel deprived. And meanwhile these questions about her mother she dare not raise; this rage at the mother for having betrayed the female potential for development; this sense of the infinite trouble that exists between mothers and daughters; these feelings she dare not acknowledge, all make it impossible for her to separate from the older woman, to go off into her own life and leave her behind. She stops, faltering before the possibilities of her own development, as she attempts frantically to unravel this complex knot that binds her energies and her ambitions.

This issue of surpassing the mother is not a simple question of doing with one's own life what the mother has not done. Rather, it is a matter of doing what the mother herself might have yearned to do and did not accomplish because of personal choice. If economic necessity or the belief in the unavoidable destiny of women shaped the mother's life, she would have had powerful aid in subduing her discontent and unhappiness with the institution of motherhood. But if the mother had alternatives and chose, nevertheless, to sacrifice herself for her daughter's sake; if she continued to feel ambivalent about this choice, yearning still for a life she did not have; if she convinced herself, now that the children had come, she could not have other forms of personal satisfaction and fulfillment, although she had already begun to doubt whether this was true; if her life continued to seethe with unacknowledged envy and resentment and muted yearning—then would her life raise for her daughter this problem of surpassing the mother that rests, I believe, at the heart of an eating problem. A daughter faces the issue of surpassing the mother when the older woman is no longer able to accept her oppression as inevitable or to efface herself as a person and to live vicariously through her child. For then the daughter, if she seeks her own development, faces two intolerable possibilities. Suddenly, in coming of age and entering the world, she is in danger of calling up the older woman's envy and resentment. And even worse, more painful and disturbing to consider, she is now in a position to remind her mother of her own failure and lack.

Who, then, is there to blame? The wounded mother, who was once a daughter? The angry daughter, who may one day, as a mother herself, become the target of her own daughter's reproach?

We must progress beyond this tendency to blame the mothers. And we must at the same time become conscious of our anger and frustration, the sense of abandonment we have all known at times, daughters of women in crisis like ourselves. And then, having lived through the shock of acknowledging our rage at the mother, we must learn how to place it in a social context, taking the personal mother out of the home and setting her in that precise historic moment in which she gave birth to a child.

Most women manage to keep their breakdown and crisis hidden so long as they remain at home and persevere in the increasingly futile struggle to make a sacrifice of themselves to marriage and maternity. The underlying crisis, however, breaks through and becomes conspicuous as soon as a woman steps out to take advantage of those social opportunities made available in our time. Thus, a woman of any age becomes a modern mother, a woman in serious if hidden crisis, when she cannot efface and sacrifice herself and live through her children. But the same woman, at any age, becomes a daughter with an eating disorder the moment she steps out to seek her own development and must pause to brood upon her mother's life.

An eating disorder can be resolved only within this largest cultural context, which allows us to rage because of how terribly we have been mothered but including now in this rage our mothers as daughters with a right to their own despair. Then we shall have liberated an anger that indicts not the mothers but a social system that has never ceased to suppress women. And we shall be able finally to set free from the tangled knot of self-destruction and obsession the radical and healing knowledge that an eating disorder is a profoundly political act.

I am describing generations of women who suffer guilt: women who cannot mother their daughters because their legitimate dreams and ambitions have not been recognized; mothers who know they have failed and cannot forgive themselves for their failure; daughters who blame themselves for needing more than the mother was able to provide, who saw and experienced the full extent of the older woman's crisis, who cannot let themselves feel rage at their mother because they know how much she needs them to forgive her.

And what becomes of all this guilt felt by the daughters? How does it come to expression? Where do we find it breaking out in a disguised and symptomatic form?

But of course we know. We have by now the answer to this question, we know how the daughters of our time are turning against themselves. We have seen the way they break down at the moment they might prosper and develop; we have observed the way they torture themselves with starvation and make their bodies their enemies, the way they attack their female flesh. This futile attack upon the female body, through which we are attempting to free ourselves from the limitations of the female role, hides a bitter warfare against the mother. The characteristic traits of an eating disorder speak to us about the guilt we feel and the hidden anger we cannot express. For what is it a woman is likely to attack if she cannot directly express her anger toward her mother? Isn't she likely, in turning this anger against herself, to direct it toward the female body she shares with her mother? In a stunning act of symbolic substitution, the daughter aims her mother-rage at her own body, so like the one which fed her and through which she learned to know the mother during the first moments of her existence.

But the female body is not the problem here. It is the guilt and anguish derived from this symbolic attack against the mother that entraps the daughter's development. Hoping to master her rage, anxiety, and sense of loss at separating from the mother by directing these feelings toward her own female flesh, the woman coming of age today involves herself in an intensified act of self-destruction at the very moment she is seeking to evolve a new sense of self.

This is the tragic paradox the new woman must resolve.

PART THREE

The Primal Feast

I

*People ask me: Why do you write about food, and eating
and drinking? Why don't you write about the struggle for
power and security, and about love, the way others do?*

*They ask it accusingly, as if it were somehow gross,
unfaithful to the honor of my craft.*

*The easiest answer is to say that, like most other humans, I
am hungry. But there is more than that. It seems to me that our
three basic needs, for food and security and love, are so mixed
and mingled and entwined that we cannot straightly think of one
without the others. So it happens that when I write of hunger, I
am really writing about love and hunger for it, and warmth and
the love of it and the hunger for it . . . and then the warmth and
richness and fine reality of hunger satisfied . . . and it is all
one.* [M. F. K. Fisher, *The Art of Eating*]

The process of unraveling, to which we boldly committed
ourselves from the first pages of this book, has brought us out
into surprising terrain. In the world of our daily life where we
rush about preoccupied with food and weight, eating and dieting, we have discovered severe crisis, breakdown, the mother's ambivalence, the daughter's despair. What is the ground
we have traveled so far, from obsession to mother/daughter
separation? It is the ground of our potential liberation.

It is important that we continue to ask the right questions, to keep our gaze fixed on underlying meanings as we follow the twists and turns of the theory's thread. If I were a reader of this book there is at this point a question I would have to raise. Why, I would wonder, does a woman in an identity crisis, caught in a mother-separation struggle, express her turmoil through food? What subterranean connection exists, still unexplored, between food, mothers, and identity?

This question fascinates me. On the one hand, the association between food and mothers is so obvious we need hardly prolong the discussion of it. For the mother is indeed, as Elias Canetti has pointed out, "one who gives her own body to be eaten. She first nourished the child in her womb and then gives it her milk." As infants, crying out from hunger and cold, from loneliness, from fear of any sort, we cried for a mother who arrived as food. And, therefore, in subsequent crises of adult life, when we are lonely and fearful because of our struggle to separate from the mother, it is only natural that we would reach toward food for the same comfort and reassurance it brought us in childhood. ("So it happens that when I write of hunger, I am really writing about love and the hunger for it, and warmth and the love of it and the hunger for it.") At this, the most obvious level of explanation, we can understand why a woman who feels that she must leave the mother behind would attempt to grasp and hold on to an object that is symbolically equivalent to the mother and has, in fact, from the first hours of existence been associated with her. If we are angry at her because of this need for separation, we can always (biting and gobbling and devouring and tearing) express this rage toward food. If we are lonely for her in these new hours of independence, we can always (sucking and sipping, soft foods and milk foods) appease this loneliness the way she always did. For isn't that, after all, what this primal association between food and mother means?

Resonating from the very deepest layers of meaning, the mother is always conjured up and made present by the presence of food. This simple idea, before we are done with it, will prove to have surprising revelations for us.

But what about the struggle for identity? Is it as evident that its various crises would tend to be expressed through our relationship to food? Why, let us wonder, do we make use of eating to reflect our often hidden, underlying dramas of development? Food and mothers may well be yoked together associatively since childhood. But food and identity?

Well, why not? Just listen, for instance, to the way Erik Erikson describes the first basic stage of conflict and resolution through which the human being passes in the struggle for identity.

> *As the newborn infant is separated from his symbiosis with the mother's body, his inborn and more or less co-ordinated ability to take in by mouth meets the mother's more or less co-ordinated ability and intention to feed him and to welcome him. At this point he lives through, and loves with, his mouth, and the mother lives through, and loves with, her breasts or whatever parts of her countenance and body convey eagerness to provide what he needs. . . . To him the mouth is the focus of a general first approach to life.*

The child who lives through and loves with the mouth is already constructing that hunger knot in which identity, the beginnings of the mother-separation struggle, love, rage, food, and the female body are entangled.

Identity, in Erikson's account of human development, does not descend to us fully formed from the gods. It is not the gift of our genes, but is rather struggled for step by step from the first moments of life. And so in this altogether heroic ascent from

symbiosis to separation we find the ego launched on an enterprise of becoming, grappling with the environment and its own
needs, faced with challenges it must meet and master in every
stage of its growth so that it may come finally to "re-emerge
from each crisis with an increased sense of inner unity." But if
it fails in any one of these progressive stages it will come to
know itself in some vital way nicked and impaired, not quite
able to trust, not fully capable of asserting its autonomous will,
lacking perhaps in initiative, finding itself deficient in enterprise, and so entering adolescence with its subsequent quest for
identity influenced by these earlier developmental battles it has
survived.

Erikson calls the first developmental stage, when the infant is
completely dependent upon the mother, Trust versus Mistrust,
to indicate the distinctive issue confronting the small child
when it first opens its mouth to howl and to receive food. If food
is brought to us in ample amounts, on a predictable schedule,
on appropriate occasions, we acquire the capacity to trust our
own needs and mother's ability to meet these needs. From this
basic trust we thereby establish our ability, or lack of ability, to
trust the world.

In the second stage of development Erikson describes, we
struggle for autonomy, the "will to be oneself." For we have
grown older by now; we have moved from that stage Freud calls
the "oral stage," in which the primary lessons we learn are associated with the sensations of the mouth, into that phase of
anal confrontation and crisis in which the child's ability to at-
tain a sense of its own "autonomous will" is mediated by the
various, sometimes violent, negotiations that take place during
toilet training.

Here, however, I would depart from Erikson's formulations,
which follow identity formation from mouth to bowels, and
then, in each successive stage of development, on out into the

world. For it seems equally evident that throughout the life of a
child, the struggle for autonomy is simultaneously taking place
through behavior directed toward food and involving the
mother as the primary giver of food. The small child asking to
be fed when it is hungry and thirsty, demanding this right
against ideas of regular meals, fretting and protesting when this
organic need is not met, has already engaged the issue of autonomous behavior long before it moves into its battle for control
of the bowels. Far, far earlier, scarcely out of its mother's arms,
it has already confronted a society's notions of appropriate
child rearing and has felt the conflict and struggle of its own imperative needs against these norms.

Indeed, it would be possible to argue, as Erikson does not,
that all the issues of development through which the child
passes between infancy and adolescence are negotiated in a
first, essential form through the relationship to food and feed-
ing. Our efforts to gain a vital sense of trust, autonomy, initiative and industry—these struggles that take us into adolescence—
are all issues that are experienced, perhaps even in their most
crucial form, by the way we are taught to conduct ourselves
with the food we eat.

Erikson describes the struggle for initiative as the child during the third year of life begins to move about freely in the
world. And yet already during that very early stage of existence
when the child first attempts to feed itself, picking up a spoon in
a little fist, grabbing a handful of mashed potatoes from the
plate, the impulse to initiate behavior on one's own behalf is already apparent. And no doubt the success or failure of one's
struggle to believe in one's own initiative has already been
strongly influenced by the way the mother responds to this repeated, earliest assertion of one's own desire. Or think of the
child, older now, expressing a preference for one food instead of
another, a liking for squash instead of spinach, a love for

oranges at the beginning of the meal instead of as dessert, a persistent inclination to eat apples day after day instead of the grapes and bananas the mother brings home. Surely here, too, in this repeated question of what shall be eaten, in what order, at what time of the day, the whole question of initiative is sounded, over and over again. The success or failure of the enterprise is strongly influenced by whether the mother manages to respect these wishes of her child or relegates them instead to a second place in her efforts to impose her own and her society's idea of what is suitable, nutritious, appropriate, and beneficial. Food presides over each of the developmental stages we pass through, offering a highly charged field of negotiation for both the mother and child.

"I know a beautiful honey-colored actress who is a gourmande, in a pleasant way," writes M. F. K. Fisher. "She loves to cook rich hot lavish meals. She does it well too. But this star-eyed slender gourmande has a daughter about eight or nine, and the daughter HATES her mother's sensuous dishes. In fact, she grows spindly on them. The only way to put meat on her bones is to send her to stay for a week or two with her grandmother, where she eats store-bought ice cream for lunch, mashed potatoes for supper, hot white pap for breakfast. 'My daughter!' the actress cries in despair and horror."

Food is never very far from our struggle to establish an identity. The sense of industry a child must learn if she is to have a vital sense of her own power must have been fought for already that first time she took a stepladder from beneath the kitchen counter, dragged it over to the shelves, and climbed up to get herself a Fig Newton—without asking her mother's approval or permission. Or we may imagine that moment she first figured out she could reach up and open the refrigerator by herself, expressing her sense that she could indeed trust the environment to meet her needs, making herself independent of her mother's will, for she is enacting an important sense of initiative and establishing her first sense of industry, as she smears a piece of bread with mustard and peanut butter and cheese. And does the older woman laugh at this absurd concoction, pat her on the head, and encourage her to eat? Does she grow upset at the food smudged and smeared on the refrigerator door, on the floor, all over the kitchen table? Does she encourage the child to repeat this effort to make things for herself, in spite of the mess involved in it all? Isn't identity being learned here, and struggled for and perhaps achieved, precisely through the relationship to food and to the mother who provides it?

"You'll sit there until you finish your meal," we say to the child who refuses to eat, without in the least realizing how potently we engage in this way a heated debate about identity. "Don't make a mess, I'll do it for you," we say when the child reaches out to mix a chocolate milk. Food is so charged, so significant, so informed with primal meaning and first impressions of life, mothering, and the world that we might well expect the communications that take place through food to carry even more weight than those that arise when a child totters about knocking into furniture or pushes a truck across the floor.

And so we come, stage by stage in this way, to adolescence, when the youth must struggle to form an image of what she is and may become. Is it a wonder, then, that she continues to express this struggle through her relationship to food?

When a woman eats by herself, vomits in secret, refuses to share food with other people in the family—these seem reasonable ways for her to express her profound sense of isolation in the struggle to become what no earlier generation has been able to imagine to this degree, on this scale, with this apparent social ease. When she cannot get on with her own development and move into normal stages of generativity and creativity, but seems rather to stagnate as she pursues the repetitive round of an eating disorder, this too seems a perfectly logical way to express a crisis in her ability to believe she has the right, as a woman, to create. Does she feel despair, instead of a sense of integrity, at being a woman in this time and place, where the struggle to evolve herself further as a fully acknowledged human being is meeting with so much opposition? And if indeed she feels despair, isn't it perfectly understandable now that she express this despair in the manner she chooses, prepares, consumes, or eliminates her food? Since childhood, food has been the most evident symbol available for expressing her struggles and failures and triumphs with an emerging sense of self.

Men, encouraged early to move away from the sphere of the mother's influence and from all those subtle, complex interactions that take place in the kitchen, at the family table, in and through food, may well need other modes and metaphors to express their various crises with identity. But when we recall the inevitable association between food and mothering; when we appreciate the way profound communications on the issue of development pass between mothers and children through the distinctive ways food is given and withheld; when we pause to consider how distinctive a form of female bonding the giving and receiving of food remains for mothers and daughters, who are not encouraged to test and know themselves outside the home, the kitchen, the family table, in the world, we will cease to wonder that the issues of female identity express themselves through food. And of course this will prove to be especially true when the problem of a woman's self-development includes, as we have seen, the important issue of separation from the mother. For the mother, from the child's first moments of existence, was an

inseparable part of the struggle for identity—as closely associated with identity as she, throughout the life of her child,
also has been associated with food.

II

In M. F. K. Fisher's autobiography, *The Gastronomical Me,*
there is an amazing illustration of the association between
food and identity, which serves as a fascinating mother/
daughter story as well. It is of course not at all surprising
that when Fisher, famous as a writer on food and the joys of
eating, came to speak directly about her own life, she presented her story through tales of memorable eating. Indeed,
I opened *The Art of Eating* at the advice of a friend because I
hoped to discover in it a few stories, an anecdote here and
there, that would help to amplify my general theme that experience with food might well be, for a girl, the essential
ground on which important lessons about her social role
might be communicated and lasting attitudes toward life
and her own being imparted. I was not disappointed. Fisher
showed herself to be a pioneer observer of the psychological
transactions that take place in the kitchen. Her tale begins
with her memory of the first taste of ''the grayish-pink fuzz
my grandmother skimmed from a spitting kettle of straw-
berry jam'' when she was four years old. Thereafter it locates
its penetrating study of identity and social life at the kitchen
stove and around the family table. It will be worth our while
to enter this narrative in some detail, for in it we can see how
deep and disturbing a mother/daughter drama can be en-

acted, over several generations, through the preparing and serving up of food.

> Women in those days made much more of a ritual of their household duties than they do now. Sometimes it was indistinguishable from a dogged if unconscious martyrdom. There were times for This, and other equally definite times for That. . . . And there were other periods, almost like festivals in that they disrupted normal life, which were observed no matter what the weather, finances, or health of the family. . . . With us, for the first years of my life, there was a series, every summer, of short but violently active cannings.

Fisher thus sets the scene for what will become a unique auto-biographical excursion, for this eloquent chronicler of fine eating is gifted also in the ability to capture the hidden tensions in family life. Within the next few pages we meet the stern, grim, religious grandmother and the youthful mother who lives under grandmother's culinary tyranny. Soon there rises before our eyes the entire world of late-Victorian domestic arrangements, along with the essential themes of childhood: the struggle between divergent life-styles, the conflict of loyalties, the tug-of-war between the generations, and the impact these make upon a growing girl, all presented in a discussion of food.

There is, for instance, the story of Ora the cook, whom Grandmother hates because she makes food pleasurable. It is a drama of conflicting wills and personalities played out around the kitchen stove. For Grandmother worries that the children will not be able to digest this food of sensual delight. "Take what God has created and eat it humbly and without sinful pleasure," Grandmother has been wont to say. But Ora the gastronomic rebel continues to serve up pie-crust stars, to the

delight of Mary Frances and her sister, and now this food subversion of Grandmother's world view causes havoc at table.
The children comment on this wondrous new food while
Grandmother frowns and frets about their manners. Food
should be eaten, she insists, without comment either of praise
or of pleasure. Now their mother is dragged into this conflict
between the austerities of spirit and the delights of flesh, "for
she after all had been raised by Grandmother." Dutiful still to
her mother's culinary philosophy, she takes the children aside
and speaks to them sternly about the need for silence where
food is concerned.

These things are important. We know that M.F.K. Fisher,
this child instructed in silence and simplicity where food was
concerned, grew up to become a famed writer about gourmet
food, an excellent cook, and a student of gastronomic lore.
Clearly, she did not take her grandmother's side in this ancient
struggle between spirit and flesh. Clearly, she was stirred,
already in childhood, by a profound response to those other influences presenting themselves at the kitchen table, where
Grandmother sat in bilious splendor eating rice water and tomatoes stewed with white bread in determined resistance to this
seduction to pleasure by Ora the cook.

But this tale of sedition in the kitchen has a sinister twist to it
that deepens it even beyond issues of identity formation and
perhaps also beyond the writer's conscious intentions. It allows
us to catch a glimpse of the mother/daughter story we have been
following. For Ora, "a spare, gray woman who kept to herself
with a firm containment," one Sunday failed to return from her
day off because she had, after a quiet church day with her own
mother, lifted that French knife of hers that had fascinated Mary
Frances and her sister. But on that day she used the knife not to
cut and carve and mince and chop, "as if it were part of her
hand," those extraordinary meals for which she was disliked and

suspected. This time the long knife, with its bright, curved point, which Grandmother had always regarded as a "wicked affectation," was employed by Ora to murder her own mother, whom she "cut into several neat pieces with the French knife."

"Anne and I were depressed," says this masterful storyteller, who must now, because of Ora's crime and subsequent suicide, be subject once again to Grandmother's grim and monotonous regimen. "The way of dying was only of passing interest to us at our ages, but our inevitable return to sensible, plain food was something to regret."

The language remains spare and laconic, but the implications of the macabre tale may be readily inferred. Nothing is said about the tension between mother and daughter that all along was present at the family table as Grandmother declared herself against sensual joy, requiring her own daughter to enforce this stricture and creating in her granddaughter a tendency to rebel against this tyranny of asceticism and to live life in full joy of the palate and in overt loyalty to matricidal Ora.

Nothing is said about the anger this young girl may have been feeling toward her mother. There is no word yet about the ambivalence that mother herself feels, caught between her children's desire for pleasure and her own mother's insistence that she force them to renounce it. But the reverberations are palpable. Ora the cook has become a shadow presence, living out the buried rages and exasperations that pass without comment at the family meals.

Interesting, then, that the very next chapter begins with the comment: "The first thing I cooked was pure poison. I made it for mother . . ."

And so we enter the girl's first experiments at cooking. But by now we should be aware that this amusing little story of her first attempt to make pudding for her mother stands in a significant relationship to Ora's crime. If we might have missed the undertone of this tale in a more casual reading, our explorations of the hidden tensions in the mother/daughter bond must open our ears to it now. For the child's loyalty to Ora tells a hidden tale about her own filial attitudes, and these unspoken threads of implication now draw the thematic tension tighter and tighter, as the tone of the telling continues to sound with all its urbane sophistication and lightness.

But let us follow the girl's experiment step by step. It began, to be sure, in adherence to tradition as she followed a recipe from her mother's best recipe book. But then, when the white milk pudding she had prepared slid onto the plate in its "obscenely pure, obscenely colorless" condition, it offended this child who had learned well from Ora's inventive sabotage of the Victorian style. Consequently, she ran off gripped, she says, by "a kind of loyalty to Ora," without telling the nurse who had supervised her cooking. She went outside and gathered ten ripe blackberries with which to decorate the plain food. She blew off the alley dust, placed the berries in a circle around the pudding, and transformed the dull little Victorian set piece into a thing of beauty.

What has been created here is, of course, far more than a quaint little tale of a girl's first dish. Set against the shadowy tale of the matricidal French knife, this first pudding served to the mother expresses even more than the girl's intense fidelity to the principle of sensual joy she was taught to renounce. The ten berries adorning the plain pudding serve up, once again, the sabotage inherent in Ora's aesthetic leanings. Twenty minutes after the mother takes the first bite, the berries of this dessert, which carries such a heavy emblematic significance, cause her to break out in "great itching red welts." They are indeed "pure poison." And this is indeed psychological gastronomy.

In both these stories beauty, sensual joy, a love of color and life, and creative bursts of rebellion against tradition carry the shadow theme of rage and rebellion against mothers, whose life-style and values are expressed also in culinary terms, through their adherence to recipe books, plain food, and silence at meals, with all this implies about their attitudes toward life in general.

And how does the mother (that weighty shaper of identity) respond to the girl's poisonous first effort at culinary art? Is she scolded for her first act of significant initiative? Is she frightened out of her wits, sent to her room in shame, made to feel guilty for her mother's allergic response, forbidden the kitchen, banished from further experimentation of this kind? Not at all. Far from it. Mother, lying there covered in compresses, assures her at once: "Don't worry sweet," she says, "it was the loveliest pudding I have ever seen."

Undoubtedly it was this response, so full of sensitivity to the child's capacity to receive deep and lasting impressions, that led the child away from the somber overtones of Ora's fate and into her own lifelong fascination with cooking. For if we remember that Fisher grew up to be a celebrated gastronomer, an excellent cook, a lover of fine food, a writer famous for her tales of eating and hunger, we have some idea how important this little childhood scene, with all its reverberating symbolic implications, must have been. This mother, without once departing from the language of eating and food, forgives her child, encourages her experimentation, and soon, indeed, joins her in this culinary venture that continues, throughout, to express a rebellion against the grandmother's asceticism. For, indeed, Grandmother finally died. The family moved to the country. They had a chicken, a cow, and "partly," says the author, "because of that and partly because Grandmother had died we began to eat more richly."

Freed from the tyranny of her own mother's oppressive fear

of food, the author's mother came into her own. "Mother, in an orgy of baking brought on probably by all the beautiful eggs and butter lying around, spent every Saturday morning making cakes." But these cakes she prepares after her mother's death continue to address themselves to the older woman and carry the old tale of rebellion and sabotage once again enacted through food. For these are no ordinary cakes that sit cooling of a Saturday afternoon. They are piled up with icings, filled with crushed almonds, chopped currants, "and an outrageous number of calories." They are beautiful cakes, works of art, and they take their place in the kitchen as statements of sensual delight and a daughter's self-assertion.

The girl and her mother, baking and cooking, chopping nuts and churning cream ("And we could have mayonnaise, rich yellow with eggs and oil, instead of the boiled dressing Grandmother's despotic bowels and stern palate called for"), contrive together to unsettle Grandmother's ghost and to strike a meaningful symbolic blow at its bilious haunting. Mother and daughter join forces. The daughter has been freed to initiate and assert herself where cooking is concerned, the mother has come forward to take over the shaping of character and the teaching of culinary skill.

For M.F.K. Fisher, identity was shaped at the kitchen stove and confirmed at the family table, through those weighty culinary communications that transpired between mother and daughter. "The stove, the bins, the cupboards, I had learned forever, make an inviolable throne room. From them I ruled; temporarily I controlled. I felt powerful, and I loved that feeling." Indeed, throughout her life, even when she herself was not planning and cooking meals, Fisher used food for the purpose of creating and establishing her identity. She used her fingers to eat shrimp at a formal meal, ignoring the silver utensils that had been set out for that purpose, and soon everyone "at the long oppressively polite table" was using his hands. She became an "orgiastic" eater and drinker when she lived in Dijon, a city characterized by its proclivity for "mass-gourmandise." There she continued to assert, against her Grandmother, the love of life, the autonomy of will, the independence, the outrageous experimentation she acquired first at the family table, in spite of the tragic fate of Ora and the French knife, the poisonous milk pudding, and her mother's early loyalty to her own mother's will. Hers is a triumphant tale of the shaping of a proud, free spirit. It is a resonant and disturbing story of the rage so often hidden in the mother/daughter bond. It is told, from first to last, through food.

III

In her life as a gastronome, M.F.K. Fisher made deliberate and conscious use of food to forge an identity that took her out of the home and into the world. Most women use food, unconsciously, to remain trapped in the home and tied to the unresolved issues of mother/daughter negotiations. For most of us, food fails to provide a symbolic sphere in which we can gradually rehearse and finally release ourselves from the snarls of the mother/daughter bond. But for us, too, food holds the potential for symbolic representation and for meaningful enactment.

The Gastronomical Me is a tour de force, to be sure. It is also like the breaking of the sound barrier or the first running of the four-minute mile. After our nurturing of countless generations, it was, I suppose, inevitable that someone finally would take food seriously enough to present it with all its weighty emblematic potency. Or is it a question not of seriousness but of shame?

Women can speak more easily about sexual fantasy and experience than they can about their eating behavior. Indeed, they can more easily speak about almost anything than about their relationship to food. The shame that informed sexual confessions at the turn of this century, when Freud began his pioneering work on the unconscious, in our time burdens the discussion of eating. The women who come to speak with me have frequently had years of therapy and analysis. They have explored hidden sexual fantasies and impressions. They have looked into the locked secrets of childhood, opened the bedroom doors and listened to the confused echoes of muffled sexual sounds. And they have never once told their analyst that every week, or after every huge meal or twice daily, they make use of laxatives or self-induced vomiting to free their body from the taint of food. Often, with surprising ease, a woman will speak about masturbating and recall her mother's response to the discovery that she had become, already as a small child, a sexual being. But rarely will the same woman be able to speak with ease about the greed and desire, the lust and yearning she feels for food. The same female body in which sexual desire is now permitted, this body long since accepted, and often celebrated, for its genital urgings, continues to fill women with alarm because of the desires that take shape in their mouth. Their body as repository of appetite fills them with shame, and they are deprived, therefore, of the meanings stored in their everyday experience of food and eating. They are unable to make metaphor and symbol from this fertile experience of daily life.

One of the indirect lessons we can learn from Fisher's densely symbolic gastronomical tale is how much, by now, we have all taken to heart Freud's emphasis on sex at the expense of other, equally potent childhood impressions. Through Freud we know a great deal about the plight of the oedipal child outside the parental bedroom, open to the reception of traumatic influences, as he listens for sounds of the primal scene. For in this psychology of early childhood elaborated by Freud and his followers, it is the fantasy of the (usually) unseen sexual act that establishes the oedipal complex, with its lasting influence upon personality and the neurotic patterns of adult identity. But Fisher's book should make us aware how thoroughly we have slighted another sphere of experience and learning, which is also rich in fantasy and mysterious impression and which reaches, moreover, in an unbroken line of influence from the mother's breast, to the kitchen table, to the adult woman's troubled relation to the food she eats. We are in the twentieth century heirs to a powerfully influential school of genital, bedroom psychology. But we are, as women at a time of profound cultural change, in need of a new psychological emphasis upon the breast and the kitchen.

For there are other questions I, as a reader of this book, would wish to raise at this point. I would hope that the "sinister implications" in the tale of Ora the matricide, from which M.F.K. Fisher's autobiography veered off, would be pursued. If there is, indeed, a hidden rage at the mother deep enough to keep us from separating successfully from her because we suffer from a pervasive feeling of guilt, surely we must uncover it. We have followed the pathway of identity formation through its association with food and mothers. But is there, as I have suggested, something we have not yet seen, something we have slighted, some earliest stage of eating and fantasy and relationship to the mother during which lasting impressions have been laid down? Is there a further connection we can make between food and mothers that will help us to explain why a woman attempting to separate from her mother, to surpass her and take on a type of development of which her mother also may have dreamed, would falter and break down?

Erikson has directed our attention to the first moments of consciousness formed at the mother's breast. But there is an entire world of fantasy, dating back to those first weeks and months of existence, which he has slighted and to which we must now turn. It is a hidden world, not easily broached. There is something about it that makes us want to turn away and avoid its implications. But in it, to be sure, are buried feelings that come to the surface in an eating disorder.

It was Melanie Klein, fascinated as she was by the pre-oedipal development of the superego in the small child, who first took Freud's fascination with childhood back to even earlier developmental stages. She was a pioneer in the field of child psychoanalysis, and "her extensive contributions, perhaps even because of their often highly controversial nature, provided an immense impetus for the study of the earliest stages of individual development and for the investigation of the primitive elements in psychic life." Indeed, in her various books and lectures, she gave a vivid and extraordinary description of the state of mind and being of infants who have not yet acquired speech. And in so doing she laid the basis for a type of psychological investigation that must concern us still today. In *The Psychoanalysis of Children,* Klein writes:

> *The idea of an infant of from six to twelve months trying to destroy its mother by every method at the disposal of its sadistic trends—with its teeth, nails, and excreta and the whole of its body—presents a horrifying, not to say an unbelievable picture to our minds. And it is difficult, as I know from my own experience, to bring oneself to recognize that such an abhorrent idea answers to the truth. But the abundance, force and multiplicity of the cruel phantasies which accompany these cravings are displayed before our eyes in early analysis so clearly and forcibly that they leave no room for doubt.*

I think we need not be overly troubled by the type of language Klein uses to describe infantile mental life. She was herself confronted, as she admits, by the rather deeply rooted repugnance this view of the small child's fantasy life seems to arouse and was, no doubt, influenced by it in her choice of language. Where she talked about cruelty and sadism we can more calmly speak of infantile frustration and anger directed at the mother and experienced (as are all other sensations and feelings of these earliest years) most forcefully through the mouth.

The milk runs more slowly than usual today. There is frustration. The little fists ball up, the face crinkles, there is that wail of rage with which every mother is familiar. The infant wakes crying at night, frightened by a sudden noise, a gust of air, a dream. The mother, also dreaming, sleeps on, exhausted by the day's toil. The fear becomes anger, the child lies wailing and thrashing. Then the anger becomes rage, the legs begin to kick, the arms flail. The mouth opens, through which it sucks and bites and devours: warmth, world, breast, milk, mother. The mouth shuts. And now like a dream the imagery comes of tearing and biting—this impotent little creature driven to fantasy because in fact it is completely helpless. It cannot bite, it has no teeth.

We must not allow Klein's language to prejudice us against her thought for she will serve us well in our efforts to uncover the seeds of this hidden mother-rage and mother-guilt, which are, at present, restricting our development. Klein speaks, for instance, about the infant's desire, or indeed its "craving, to scoop and suck out . . . and devour all the fluids and other substances which its parents . . . contain." She mentions the "oral-sadistic phantasies" of early childhood, "which seem to form a link between the oral-sucking and oral-biting stages" and which have, she says, a "quite definite character, and contain ideas that he gets possession of the contents of his mother's breast by sucking and scooping it out." She claims that "this desire to suck and scoop out, first directed to [the mother's] breast, soon extends to the inside of her body." She describes an early stage of the child's development that is "governed by the child's aggressive trends against its mother's body and in which its predominant wish is to rob her body of its contents and destroy it." She goes on to assure us, in *Love, Guilt and Reparation,* that in fact the child feels that "what he has desired in his phantasies has really taken place; that is to say he feels that he *has really destroyed* the object of his destructive impulses, and is going on destroying it." And, finally, she concludes this discussion with the idea that "these basic conflicts profoundly influence the course and the force of the emotional lives of individuals."

Perhaps then it is not surprising that when certain needs, reminiscent of childhood, make themselves felt in adult life, they take a disguised form. Rage at the mother, or at life in general; a desire to have needs satisfied by another who cannot meet these needs; a necessity to separate from one's mother literally in adolescence, or symbolically at any later stages in life—all may hold the power of awakening again these frightening oral rages the infant experienced. Little surprise, therefore, that what we feel of rage and need and frustration and desire; or of anguish and loneliness; or of guilt and remorse and dismay, we express through our disguising relationship with food. After all, that mother whom Melanie Klein evokes was to the small child, as we have seen, indistinguishable from food—as she lifted us and placed us at her breast to feed us.

Any woman with an eating problem, anyone indeed who knows anyone with an eating problem, must be familiar with the extremes of anxiety, guilt, and remorse that characterize a disordered relationship to food. But I wish to suggest that we have not known exactly how to account for the extremity of these feelings because we have neglected the Kleinian fantasy life of the pre-oedipal infant.

Therefore, let us now hypothesize. Underlying the symptomatology of an eating disorder—whether anorexia, bulimia, or the type of sustained, unpurged, compulsive eating that may lead to obesity—is this unconscious "Kleinian memory"—a wish to bite and tear at the mother, to scoop and suck out her fluids, with the concomitant belief that one has really done this and has consequently damaged the mother, drained her, depleted her, and sucked her dry. I wish, in all earnestness, to suggest that we can understand the self-destructiveness of eating problems only by relating them to a girl's belief that long ago, in earliest childhood, she inflicted this type of oral attack upon her mother and succeeded in depleting her.

It may be that Freud is correct and that our most fruitful understanding of male psychology comes to us from an exploration of the oedipal situation. For a man to develop into full manhood he must, according to Freud, surmount the guilt that arises from his fantasy of destroying his father in order to obtain possession of his mother. But our most fruitful understanding of female psychology will come from the exploration of the dual-unity, mother and child, mouth-to-breast dyad of earliest childhood, which implies that for a woman to develop into her full womanhood she must surmount the guilt that arises from her fantasy of having damaged the mother through the force of her oral aggression and rage.

For Melanie Klein these infantile fantasies of oral aggression have a quality of inexorable doom—they are produced regardless of circumstance by the inevitable frustrations of infantile life. But I would suggest, in disagreement with this view, that in this earliest stage of development, along with the frustration and rage felt when primal needs are not immediately met, there will be for an infant the continual reassurance of the mother's power, presented most vividly to the mind of a small child through the ever-replenishing quality of the mother's milk. We may rage and attack, we may bite at her in reality and tear at her in fantasy, but the food supply on which our life depends continues to reconstitute itself. And this of course will be true for the child fed by the bottle as well. No clear separation has yet been made between what the mother is and what she does. She who feeds us is the food we eat. And therefore at this stage our frustrations and rages need not yet seem dangerous or catastrophic to us, because the mother continues to produce and offer food in spite of our attacks. She remains whole.

But now we imagine that the child is growing up a little. She has come to the time of weaning, a first, formidable separation from the mother. I wish us here to imagine how this event might look to a small being who is developing in the shadow of these aggressive oral fantasies we have been discussing, for we know that childhood concepts are powerfully shaped by the physical experiences in which they arise. And now I suggest that a child who has sucked away at the mother, raged at her in fantasy and bitten at her in reality, will very likely come to believe that she is being weaned, and separated from the mother, because she has finally depleted her and drained her dry.

We must recall that as the child continues to grow the vision of an all-powerful mother gradually fades. As the needs of the infant become more complex and demand a more highly complicated response from the mother, her failings and difficulties as a mother become more apparent. And soon there comes before the child, in place of the omnipotent magical mother of infancy, the mother in reality—a woman who is, let us say, in conflict about maternity, longing for a self-development that she has not achieved and that the birth of a child will make even more elusive, a woman frequently harassed, sometimes depressed, often distraught. Where once she was able to bring magical relief to so many of our needs (ending darkness, dispelling terror, soothing hunger, banishing cold), she increasingly appears to us as a person who has difficulty taking care of us and maybe even problems caring for herself.

This sensitivity to the mother is not at all beyond the capacity of even a very young child. Psychologists studying the earliest relations between mother and child speak of the "quasi-telepathic communication between mother and infant as being of a 'co-enesthetic type,' wherein sensing is visceral and stimuli are 'received' as opposed to being 'perceived.' The mother's affective state is 'received' by the infant and is registered in the form of emotions." Infants feel what their mothers are feeling.

And so we come upon what is in fact a highly unfortunate concatenation of events: the food supply running out while at the same time the mother seems to be diminishing in stature and power as the child grows. We can easily imagine now that a small child, whose emotional life is strongly dominated by fantasies of aggression against this mother, would be likely to blame herself for what seems to be the mother's terrible diminishment. In the self-referring causality of childhood fantasy an inevitable confusion arises, and three false conclusions are drawn. In the first place: the food has ceased because of our oral aggression against the mother. Furthermore: the draining away of this vital substance has caused damage to the mother. And finally: our growth and development have involved the diminishment of the mother.

I suggest that in our attempt to understand the relationship between eating disorder and female identity crisis we must recognize that these three false conclusions play a fateful and essential role. From the very origins of identity at the mother's breast they establish a predisposition to guilt about one's own growth and development, which is seen against a background of another's diminishment and depletion. And they suggest the likelihood that these preoccupations and concerns would continue to express themselves in our relationship to food.

But wait, let us slow down, let us go much more slowly indeed. To what are we committing ourselves with this view of infantile life? To the notion that these earliest fantasies now determine the shape of adult life, unrelentingly? I think not. But we can easily imagine that they would leave a mark, a receptivity to other impressions of a similar sort. Or they might incline us to interpret later events so that they seem to confirm our earlier surmise. It is not that we *think* we have harmed the mother with our biting and chewing and devouring. It is rather that these wrathful fantasies, born of our frustration and impotence, leave behind a fertile soil in which later events cast their seed. When a more mature emotional life has been built up, we worry about the people we love. We fear our anger toward them and fear to harm them with our rage and feel guilt when we have grabbed at mother's hair and tugged it in our fists. And later that day, when she was putting us to bed, she seemed weary perhaps. Seeing that pale look crossing her face, we put our arms around her neck and murmured "Don't be sad, Mama, don't be sad." Then can we imagine that the child's sense of this weariness in the mother will be influenced by those half-formed, lingering fantasies of infantile biting at this woman who did not come when we called out to her.

Here, indeed, we may observe the way apparently inevitable stages of childhood development and fantasy are profoundly influenced by social institutions. For we can easily imagine that a hale and hearty woman, fulfilled and happy in her life and able, let us say, to combine career and family with her own personal quest for fulfillment and identity, will be profoundly reassuring to her child. The fear of having sucked her dry and depleted her will be offset by the evidence of her prospering reality. The terrible fear of damaging her through our aggression will be reassured by her radiant well-being. But in fact, for most of us, our worst fears of damaging our mother are enhanced by what we come to know of the realities of her life and conflicts.

We can readily imagine what it will mean to a child whose

emotional life is strongly influenced by fantasies of oral aggression if the mother shares this same image of maternity—if she in fact feels drained or depleted or exhausted by the child's needs and cannot help but communicate this to her child, who is already strongly predisposed to take this message literally, as an actual draining and depleting of the vital resources of the mother. How fatefully here childhood fantasy, developmental inevitability, and the particular institutions of mothering a culture evolves work together, through the personality of an individual woman, to impress upon a little child the message that as she flourishes her mother inevitably declines. Since she blames her oral aggression for sucking the mother dry, she inevitably begins to feel profoundly guilty—not only about her growth and development, but about her eating as well.

In the women with severe and debilitating eating disorders who have come to speak with me there are, consistently, these underlying features: a daughter at a developmental turning point who is required, at least symbolically, and usually literally as well, to separate further from her mother; a daughter whose fantasy life is dominated by this notion of having sucked the mother dry, drained, exhausted, and depleted her; a mother who communicates to her daughter that she is, in reality, drained, exhausted, depleted, not up to the task of mothering, and frequently not up to the crises of her own life; a culture that sets the institution of motherhood apart from a woman's quest for identity, so that both mother and daughter experience their relationship as damaging to the mother and as one that deprives her of self-development.

It is, of course, a vicious circle. A woman who has not been allowed or encouraged to develop herself as a person becomes a depleted mother whose inability to meet her child's needs produces frustration and an intense degree of oral rage, which then breed the wrathful fantasy of attacking the mother, draining and depleting her, to get at her vital source. And then this fantasy is apparently confirmed by what the daughter learns of her mother's exhaustion and depletion in reality. It seems virtually inevitable that this daughter would conclude, "I did this thing, I through my rage and need have brought my mother to this harm." The terrible guilt we see in a woman with an eating disorder, although it is usually focused on the number of calories consumed and the number of pounds gained, arises from the fact that the woman afflicted with this obsession cannot forgive herself for having damaged her mother in earliest childhood. Consequently, she cannot allow herself to move into the next stages of development, to turn her back on the older woman and leave her behind to the depletion and exhaustion she believes she has inflicted upon her.

Now, finally, we can understand why eating disorders have become so prominent in our time. For in a generation where daughters are offered the opportunity to take their growth and development past that which was available to their mothers, we would expect daughters to feel the full force of that early childhood guilt about damaging the mother and deriving their growth and development at the expense of hers. If, as their mothers before them, they simply followed in their mothers' footsteps, they would give up the longing for their own development and sacrifice it for their children. And thus the whole cycle would be avoided—the attempt to surpass, which calls up the guilt of damaging, which reawakens the violent infantile fantasy, which arose from the social and psychological conditions in which mothers raise their children—the whole, endless round returning fatefully to entrap the women of our time when they must separate from their mothers and get on with their lives.

We may at this point begin to wonder why girls develop eating obsessions to express this conflict while boys seem to go free. After all, children of both sexes harbor intense oral aggressive fantasies about their mothers and would therefore be expected to hold themselves responsible for whatever damage they later come to experience in their mothers' lives. Why is it, then, that boys seem better able to forgive themselves for their early aggression while girls are stricken with remorse and a debilitating sense of guilt?

To answer this question it will be necessary to call back once again the idea of self-sacrifice that we as a culture associate with the institution of maternity. We recall, moreover, that from their earliest years both girls and boys are exposed to this idea as part of their gender training, even today when few women can wholeheartedly embrace any longer this notion of motherhood as sacrifice. Through this training we impart to the boy the knowledge that he will become like his father, independent, autonomous, involved in the world. To the girl we offer the certain promise that she, like her mother, will raise children and will sacrifice her other desires and ambitions in order to devote herself entirely to mothering. The mother, ambivalent about her own life, struggling to deny her sense of personal failure and frustration, in order to reassure herself that she could not have made other choices, may insist with especial vehemence, even when she doubts its truth, that women must sacrifice themselves for their children's sake. Daughters raised by mothers deeply in conflict about being mothers may have heard these ideological statements from their earliest years.

Boys have every reason to subscribe to this idea of maternity. It does not affect their own life choices, because these ideas about motherhood need not become part of their identity. And therefore this cultural sense of motherhood as sacrifice can help to free boys from a feeling of personal responsibility for what has happened to their mothers in mothering them. A boy able to take refuge in this idea can reassure himself that the woman, as mother, wished to make this sacrifice of herself, was fated to it by biological destiny, driven to it by some inherent instinctual force, and no doubt receives from it some kind of "higher," even mystical fulfillment.

This relief from personal responsibility for the mother's fate may be one reason men are so reluctant to give up their traditional views of woman's nature. Should a woman become a person in her own right, with a self-meaning and destiny outside the instinctual realm, men too might have to take quite personally the damage of women through the institution of motherhood. And they too might well become prey to a serious sense of guilt for the (imagined) damage they inflicted upon their mothers through their oral aggression in childhood.

In this respect, the daughter faces a far more complex developmental problem than the son. If she, in the fullness of her possibilities, cannot adopt this idea of woman's necessary sacrifice, if she challenges it or protests against it, she will be left with a restless sense of personal responsibility and severe guilt for what she did to the mother. But if, on the other hand, she attempts to offset her guilt by ascribing to this ideology of maternity, she embraces a fateful destiny for herself. Seen through the distorting lens of the infantile fantasy of eating up the mother, the idea of sacrifice ceases to be either ideological or abstract. In the imagination of the growing girl it becomes the horrifying image of the mother as literal food sacrifice. Since the daughter is a woman, too, she must fear that when she grows older she will become the mother drained and exhausted by her infants, she who is served up at the primal feast. As a woman she is caught between this dreaded sacrificial possibility and the equally dreadful sense of daughter-guilt.

The girl on a diet longs to have the body of a boy? The woman standing before a mirror feels despair when her hips no longer fit into the tight, zip-front pants? Do we see now another reason this might be so? The dread of this sacrificial possibility, which lurks in the institution of motherhood as it is still practiced in this culture, might well incline a young woman to yearn ardently to be a boy—one for whom the necessity of becoming the food sacrifice has never been a cultural expectation.

There is a sleeping giant in the female psyche, a potential for great power and potency and self-expression. At present it is entangled with the mother-rage, which for a woman so easily ends up directed at the self, out of a profound sense of kinship with the mother, a feeling of shared identity, of compassion for her plight, and from the dread of one day becoming the mother toward whom primal rage will be directed.

Here we must say something about the psychological difference between the concerted attack upon the female body evident in an eating disorder (where the body is starved and deprived of its flesh and restricted in its appetites and loathed for its abundance) and the kind of attack, in sexual fantasy or pornographic imagery or actual rape, directed by men against women. It is, of course, highly relevant that women turning aggression from the mother's body toward their own are involved in an act of self-destruction. They are, moreover, holding on to the vulnerability of the original infantile situation, in which the child rested in helpless dependency within the arms of the all-powerful mother. The woman with a food obsession continues to experience the helplessness and the overwhelming need which characterize the infant at the mother's breast and give rise to the primal rage the woman experiences all over again whenever she must separate from the mother.

But in the male act of sexual aggression against women, or in the fantasy of such aggression, primal rage is directed out and away from the self, as it takes an obsessive focus upon the female body. Now, moreover, the infantile power relations have been reversed. The original mother/child dyad is effaced and in its place comes the aggressive sexual male in a role of dominance and power. One reason men do not develop eating disorders and open themselves to that oral helplessness and vulnerability and rage is quite simply that they have available to them a far more reassuring form of obsessive attack upon the female body in their actual and imagined sexual relationship to women. And this is of course one further reason women might envy men and long to pass their lives within the male body: then their rage at the mother and at the female body would necessarily be turned away from themselves.

We must register a due regard for this striking difference between women and men. The male ability to discharge primal rage at the mother through aggressive fantasies of attack upon the female body, without at the same time incurring the danger of attacking the self, clearly gives men a powerful advantage in managing rage. And it frees them from the intensity of self-destructive behavior that arises so conspicuously at the turning point of a woman's life.

If boys were less able to experience their mother-rage through acts of sexual domination over women, and through the entire social system of female suppression, they too might require some other form of enactment in which rage and violence, need and helplessness, despair and guilt and the whole troubled history of the mother/child bond are directed against themselves.

Then they, too, might develop eating disorders.

IV

AN EATING OBSESSION COMES into existence so that the need, rage, and violence of the mother/daughter bond can be played out in a symbolic form that spares the mother. That is the basic idea we must grasp if we are to appreciate the reasons an eating obsession has such tenacious hold upon self-development.

At a turning point in a woman's life, when she is struggling to separate from her mother, we would expect her to feel the same need and frustration, rage and ambivalence she felt as a small child in all the early acts of union and separation that began at the mother's breast and through which she struggled to know herself as an autonomous being. Therefore, it is not surprising that in this crisis of her adult life she turns to food as a means of expressing the separation struggle. Through her relationship to food she can live out the earliest bonding issues with the mother—the need to incorporate the mother and to remain one with her and simultaneously in fantasy to attack and destroy her as a symbolic means of making separation possible.

If a woman at a developmental turning point could manage actually to move out into her life and confront her hidden turmoil, ambivalence, and guilt, she would not need a disguising symptomatic system through which she can unconsciously continue to enact the hidden concerns and fantasies that are troubling her. If, on the other hand, she is paralyzed by conflict and unable to become aware of what she feels, the development of symptomatology is likely.

Most women afflicted with an obsessive need to diet and eat are aware that an eating disorder contains the following seven elements: (1) an intense and driven need for food; (2) a fear about the size of the appetite; (3) a dread of eating; (4) a sense of shame about the act of eating; (5) a conspicuous feeling of guilt; (6) a dread of the body growing fat; (7) a need to diet or purge and starve.

These seven elements, although in different degrees of severity, are common to all types of eating problems. They are the essential elements that constitute the obsession. Now, however, if we want to understand the way they work for a woman in severe conflict about mother-separation and mother-surpassing, we have to translate these obsessive preoccupations into their original meaning.

(1) At the most general level we can say that in an eating obsession food has taken the place of the mother. We are now in a position to understand this symbolic equation since we have seen how the mother was, to the small infant, inseparable from food.

(2) Inevitably, then, given the filial story we have just uncovered, we would associate the fear of appetite with a woman's fear of her needs in general but more specifically with the rage that comes to expression through the mouth. For the woman in the grips of an obsessive need to eat, fear of hunger is a fear of experiencing the hidden violence in the mother/daughter bond.

(3) Similarly, we can now see that the woman's dread of eating is the form through which she experiences her dread of enacting the rage that comes to expression through her hunger. This equation also would seem easy to understand because the infant's early oral aggression was expressed during the act of

eating—both in fantasy and in the reality of infantile sucking and biting at the mother's breast.

(4) Consequently, the sense of shame the woman feels about her eating, which drives her to eat in secret, reveals that her unconscious sense of what she is doing as she eats is to reenact the old fantasy of taking in vital substance from her mother and damaging her through the aggressive force of her need and frustration. Every time she eats compulsively, in a frantic and driven way, she is unconsciously experiencing the old mother/child situation that has played so formative a role in her development. The shame she feels is the dread of being exposed as one who carries and enacts this secret aggression against the mother.

(5) And now, of course, we can understand her guilt when she compulsively devours far more food than her biological needs require. In her emotional experience, as she eats, the act of eating has become an act of violence against the mother, whom she fears she is simultaneously incorporating and damaging all over again at this moment of her life when she longs to be free from her but feels too guilty to be able to break away from the old bond.

(6) Thus, we can see also how her dread of her body growing fat is her fear that this guilty and shameful cannibalistic behavior will become apparent in her flesh; and that, through her fat body, she will be known and recognized for this reenacted primal crime. We can see how a culture that fears and dislikes large women will continually reinforce her sense of uneasiness about her body's size. For she already feels "fat" and "loathsome" when she gains weight and hates her body for bearing witness to her oral misdeeds.

(7) And so, finally, we realize that her dieting and starvation and purging and reduction of her female body are all ways of undoing this primal crime that haunts and obsesses her.

Through her diet she renounces her longing for food and for her mother; she proves her control over her oral aggression; she makes a sacrifice of her sensual appetites; she gives herself a slender, "pure" body to take the place of the fat, "guilty" one and is thus enabled to punish herself, through her hunger and starvation, for the crime of devouring her mother.

But of course we grasp at once the trap that is lying in wait for her here. For this chronic dieting and starvation leads to a great sense of oral frustration and hunger. The frustration intensifies and augments her rage. The rage leads to fantasies of oral attack against the mother (the first giver and withholder of food). The fantasies of attack call up the archaic imagery of devouring and damaging the mother. The more she starves the more she hungers, the more she rages the more she is overwhelmed with guilt. She has reproduced the primal situation perfectly. She has managed, through her eating obsession, to repeat the old drama of her infancy, with all its frustrated need and rage, symbolically through her relationship to food. Now, over and over again, she devours the mother with every mouthful of food she consumes compulsively. She feels guilty and undoes this, and then she does it all over again.

Not all eating is experienced in this way. But what is called "compulsive eating" or "the binge"—this eating which seems urgent and terrifying to the woman involved in it—must be understood as the reemergence into adult life of this archaic childhood fantasy, with all its accompanying guilt and remorse.

We must stop using the words *eating disorder* to distance ourselves from the severity of the existential problem women face in the struggle to become. Only then will we grasp fully what it means to rush home after a day of work feeling that one has been driven by a nameless urge that cannot rest and will give one no peace and that compels one to act in a way abhorrent to one's dignity and pride and for which one will subsequently entertain the most severe remorse, guilt, and self-loathing until at last one is driven to purge oneself, to diet and fast, to impose severe penance upon one's flesh before the guilt abates and one feels temporarily released from this urgency.

We can imagine this reenactment of the primal feast—the speed of the eating, the amount of food consumed, the fact that one gobbles rather than chews, bolting down the forbidden repast. At first there is an extraordinary release of tension. The need-rage one has been trying to fight down can finally be enacted. One can grab up a pound of cheese and tear off chunks of it. One can pull the breast from a chicken, gobble it practically without chewing, swallow down large hunks of flesh. One can break the bones and crunch at them and bite them clean, eating off sinew and ligament and cartilage. One can suck the marrow from them and toss them aside. One can stand at the refrigerator hacking away at a leg of lamb, the blood of which has congealed on the platter to a solid red mass. (And how much vegetarianism, one might wonder, derives from the ease with which animal flesh can be associated with human flesh and thereby lead back to the archaic fantasy of tearing and biting and devouring the mother?) The woman in her kitchen, stuffing food down her throat, is caught in a frenzy of reenactment. She feels helpless, she feels out of control, she feels that she has been taken over by an inner urge that shames and terrifies her and makes her feel profoundly guilty. She experiences this guilt as a dislike for her body; she experiences her fear as a fear of appetite. She attempts to control the entire experience by subjecting herself to the reassurance of measurable pounds and inches. But underneath this obsessive worry and concern with the body and its hungers we can detect the old cannibalistic fantasy and its forgotten urgencies and guilts and shames. The very size and persistence of her shame and guilt tell us that these cannot possibly be about her eating, even about her compulsive eating, unless that behavior is accompanied by some dreadful sense of what she is doing in imagination as she bites and gobbles and tears and breaks bones.

Do we wonder now that a woman would feel inclined to race into the bathroom and gulp down glasses of water and lean over the toilet and make herself vomit up this terrifying meal she has just eaten? Do we wonder if she takes 144 laxatives a day to purge what she imagines is a criminal repast, to move it through her body as quickly as possible and get rid of it? Are we surprised now that if she manages to tolerate the meal inside herself long enough to digest it, she makes busy plans for atonement and works out fasts and exercises that will help her undo her guilty deed? Or, if she cannot starve and purge herself, perhaps we understand now why she hides her body under loose clothes, is ashamed to look at it at night or in a bath, distances herself from it, disembodies herself, pretends the body isn't there, hurries into bed at night so that her lover cannot observe her flesh—this flesh that shames her with its curves and swelling, which may reveal the guilty secret and let the archaic fantasy become known. Her body has become evidence of the cannibal meal. Growing larger and fuller, swelling with the mother-food she has taken into it, it stands to condemn her for her guilty deed.

"Lord of the world," prayed Rabbi Sheshet of ancient times, "when the temple was standing, one who sinned offered a sacrifice of which only the fat and blood were taken, and thereby his sins were forgiven. I have fasted today, and through this fasting my blood and my fat have been decreased. Deign to look upon the part of my blood and fat which I have lost through my fasting as if I had offered it to Thee, and forgive my sins in return."

In a secular age, when the concept of sin would seem to have lost its power, a woman stripping her body of flesh performs through this offering up of fat the ritual practiced by the early Hebrews for atonement of sins. And what exactly is this imagined sin for which she is atoning? But of course we know by now. It is the crime of matricide.

We have, as a culture, grown used to the idea of associating fantasies of aggression with sexuality. In the oedipal fantasy, as Freud has conceived it, a very young child imagines acts of violence against a beloved parent, who is seen as rival and competitor for the mother's favors. We understand that this infantile fantasy reappears also in the sexual relations and desires of the adult male. If the association between eating and matricidal fantasy strikes us as especially horrifying (or absurd), this is because the fantasy of killing the mother goes back to earlier, even more tumultuous, and far more chaotic childhood experiences than the ones Freud described.

Freud led us back to the oedipal triangle and abandoned us there. But the work of Melanie Klein has allowed us to forge a link, which she too overlooked, between adult eating behavior and primal experience. Now we can grasp the association not only between infantile sexual fantasy and adult life, but between the child at the breast and the woman at a turning point. We should, however, be aware that this abstract association we piece together analytically, the body and the mouth have already forged for us in our concrete experience.

Women who eat compulsively (and countless women as well who experience only a vague sense of uneasiness when they eat) have made their bodies the recipient of feelings they cannot bear to hold in consciousness. Their rage is expressed through their mouths, their need for love and solace is experienced as a longing for food, their guilt comes to them as a feeling of fatness, their shame is transmuted into a sense of dislike for their bodies, their need for penance and absolution is expressed through self-starvation, their sacrificial offering of themselves to the mother is made through a breakdown that involves hunger and eating, mouth and flesh. Therefore, it is to the body we must turn to uncover these lost feelings and imaginative constellations.

We are in a quiet room. Trust has been established here. The sounds of daily life have retreated. The door is locked, keeping out the possibility of intrusion. Here one might hazard the perils of becoming conscious.

"Close your eyes," I say. "Observe that tightness in the jaw. Enter in imagination into that constriction."

She focuses upon the tightness in the jaws, feels from inside the force with which she grinds her teeth at night, experiences the pain and pressure, in silence holds awareness of these sensations until, finally, after many attempts at such observation, she becomes aware of a desire to bite and rip and tear with her jaws.

Her eyes fly open. She is terrified. She wants, she says, to stand up and run from the room. She is searching my face. Am I afraid of her? Am I terrified of what she is feeling? Can I see this through with her? Am I also afraid to know?

"Tell me," I say, "what is it you want to bite and rip and tear?"

She does not answer. She turns away. She makes a fist and pounds it against her thigh.

But this is a woman who never experiences anger. This is a woman who wears a splint at night to keep herself from the awful pain of grinding her teeth. This is a woman who does not know, she claims, what it is like to hate. This is a woman whose rage lives in her jaws.

Another woman. She has a reflective turn of mind. She imagines the consequences of taking into oneself an object (food) that one equates symbolically with the mother. For once the food enters the body (we reason) carrying the eater's rage and the mother's failure, the woman has inside herself every-thing of which she is most terrified. Originally, she reached out to food as for a symbolic substitution, to spare the mother from this filial aggression and to avoid her own feelings through this act of "swallowing her need and rage." But now of course she is panic-stricken by what she has done; she feels stuffed and bloated, invaded by her own rage and by the mother's imag-ined suffering and retaliatory wrath.

Another woman, following the same line of thought, has be-come conscious of the "knot" in her stomach and manages to concentrate upon this sensation of tension until it becomes a "wringing of hands."

"Wring your hands," I say to her.

"But I don't know how."

"Whose hands are these then? Who have you seen wringing hands?"

They are, she says, the hands of her mother.

As if she had swallowed up the mother's despair and kept it inside her?

She keeps her eyes closed, frowning as she concentrates upon this strange sensation in her stomach. Finally she nods her head, opens her eyes, and admits it more to herself than to me: this woman, who cut her mother out of her life more than thirty years ago, has been carrying her around, inside her, in her stomach.

For some women the mother they have taken into them-selves, along with the food they have eaten in wrath, becomes the revenge-mother, angry at them for their need of her, angry at them for their attack on her, angry at them for the way they have deprived her of life or accepted her sacrifice. She is the mother of envy and resentment who comes at them through their bodies. She is their "fat," she invades their flesh, she seethes and ferments in their bellies. Constipation (they discover), water retention, the delusions of fatness in gaunt and emaciated women, the hysterical symptoms of swelling and bloating in women of normal size, all reveal themselves as the terrifying sense that the woman has been taken over by the mother from whom she is trying to separate and whom she has swallowed down, over and over again symbolically in the reenacted primal feast, along with her own rage and need and yearning and desire and resentment and frustration, along with her food.

Now, slowly, we come to understand that *fat* means this sense of oneself taken back by the revenge-mother; it means the daughter ugly, unacceptable, rejectable, disgusting, outcast for the crime of matricide. Now, piece by piece, we come to see how food has ceased to be a purely inanimate object, a benign source of pleasure and satisfaction, and has been charged instead with the mother's qualities the child wished either to absorb or attack and with the child's own needs and aggressions. Finally, now, we see how eating has become an enactment of the primal feast—a highly charged symbolic drama of mother/daughter separation and reunion.

V

FEW WOMEN HAVE THE capacity, without lengthy preparation, to descend far enough into themselves to uncover the infantile rage and guilt that may well exist at the very foundations of consciousness, preserving there the history of the original dyad. But the kitchen of childhood provides a later sphere of memory, closely related to the nursery and the breast, where lasting impressions of the mother/daughter drama have been recorded. For the memories stored in our associations to food are a record not only of rage and aggression and troubling fantasies of oral attack. Food is emblematic also of the intense pleasure of infantile satisfaction at the mother's breast and for many later stages of experience with the mother. Just as food accompanied our acquisition of identity and served to communicate important messages about gender and social role, it presided also over highly significant encounters from later childhood, when the mother and daughter engaged one another in ways that reflected their earliest, long-forgotten first rapport. Consequently, if we do the work of reclaiming these memories from our later experience of food and mothers, we may be able to ease our way into that primal rage we have been discussing in order finally, by knowing and acknowledging, to free ourselves from it.

In hours when it is difficult for a woman to talk, when her

thoughts, turning toward childhood and her relationship to her mother, seem to hesitate and balk and then draw back, as if she had reached out to touch a hot stove and were retreating in pain and terror, I have found that there is a way to ease this passage into memory. I ask the woman to talk about the kitchen of her childhood.

It is amazing to experience the change of atmosphere in the consultation room when women are asked to tell me the first foods they remember eating or about their favorite foods in childhood or about their first efforts to prepare a little meal for themselves. The taut, strained look eases from their face, clenched hands unfold, eyes brighten.. There is laughter, a sense of joyous release. The conversation flows again, the weighty abstractions about identity and mother-separation settle into concrete form, they embody themselves. A woman remembers the way she loved oranges. She talks about sneaking into the kitchen to eat them when her mother was on the phone. She remembers eating an entire bowl of oranges when she was three years old. It is, she says, her earliest memory. With the taste of the orange consciousness has begun. She is elated to have recovered her childhood like this in memory of the taste of food. And now, when the memory itself grows more somber, when other missing pieces of childhood suddenly fall into place, she seems willing to endure them.

This increased willingness to tolerate the difficult is one of the advantages we shall derive when we use our relationship to food as a means of self-exploration. For the essential ambivalence that haunts our experience with food can serve us greatly here, letting us profit from our positive associations so that we may endure the gradual descent into those memories that rest in their thematic neighborhood but are far more disturbing.

The woman remembers: she recalls the way she would grab for the oranges out of the huge cornucopia of the brown paper bag left unattended for a moment. And now the struggle between mother and child rises vividly, dramatically, unmistakably before the woman's eyes. She recalls, with fear suddenly, that same fear of her mother she could never before remember, the way her mother reached out to slap her hand, grabbed her by the shoulders, shook her violently, exasperated by this persistent greed: "Didn't I tell you to wait for dinner? Didn't I tell you you have to share? Didn't I tell you not to stuff yourself like that?" She remembers being lifted and carried, her feet dangling off the ground; she remembers being dropped down on her bed in her room; she remembers her mother's face, "flushed and violent; it was terrible . . . that look in her eyes." She recalls how often, as a child, she was terrified of this expression, this "thing I saw there; I didn't know what it was." The memory fades suddenly. She looks puzzled, astonished. "Where did it all go? Is that," she asks, looking at me with consternation, "what happens to things you don't want to recall?"

"Do you remember what oranges taste like? Can you close your eyes and remember the taste?"

She breathes deeply; I see the rapid movement of her eyes behind closed lids; and now she smiles grimly, moving her mouth as if she is eating. "I remember how stubborn I was. Would you believe it? I was that terrified of my mother. But every chance I got, I sneaked into the kitchen and stole the oranges. I didn't always get caught. Sometimes I got away with it." Here, she looks as if she is going to cry; briefly, a look of terror passes across her face, and this time is replaced by a flush of indignation and stubborn determination. "But I kept at it; she never beat me off from those oranges."

For every woman who can speak easily about the mother of her childhood there are two or three who seem to have whitewashed those years or who find themselves unable to remember early encounters or engagements with the older woman. Many claim to be indifferent to her, to have separated from her early and completely, without looking back. Others live in a sustained illusion of unbroken early harmony and bliss. And always, listening to them, one has the impression there is more to it, something further back, different in kind, forbidden to memory and locked away beyond our familiar associative techniques, eluding our understanding of dreams, escaping the subtleties of our conjectures and analyses, resisting us however much we lie in wait for understanding.

All our ambushes fail. Even our silence remains empty and unrewarded. There is frustration in the room. They are confused by my sense that we must go further. I am busily counseling myself to proceed slowly, to remain patient. It is that strained, difficult, fretful time when the work slows down and seems virtually to stop. And then one day we happen to talk about childhood preferences and disinclinations where food was concerned, and suddenly the lost pathway back into childhood reveals itself. For this is, indeed, one of the many implications that can be drawn from the association between mothers, identity, and food. Just as sexual fantasy and memory lead back to that oedipal triangle, with its hidden jealousies and rages and forbidden desires, the memory of childhood food has the capacity to take us back to the often hidden memories of mother/daughter conflict and those formative encounters that continue to inform our efforts to become ourselves. From the taste of oranges comes the lost memory of embattled wills. And now suddenly the woman understands her "inexplicable aversion" to oranges, the rashes they cause, the strange longing, nevertheless, that often sets upon her, tearing her thoughts from her work or from a favorite book, to set her off "prowling about the kitchen," looking for "something tart, something sour, something citrus."

"As if you were about to remember something? As if you were trying to remember?"

Her eyes fill with tears; food is memory. She nods, astonished. She has been eating in order to remember.

The capacity of food to hold memory. If psychology has not made of this conjuring power of food as much as it might, literature on the other hand has been its diligent observer. Here is Golda Meir, as an old woman, remembering her childhood in the shtetl:

> There was never enough of anything, not food, not warm clothing, not heat at home. I was always a little too cold outside and a little too empty inside. Even now, from that very distant past, I can summon up with no effort at all, almost intact, the picture of myself sitting in tears in the kitchen, watching my mother feed some of the gruel that rightfully belonged to me to my younger sister, Zipke. Gruel was a great luxury in our home in those days, and I bitterly resented having to share any of it, even with the baby. Years later I was to experience the dread of my own children's hunger and to learn for myself what it is like to have to decide which child is to receive more food, but, of course, in that kitchen in Kiev, I knew only that life was hard and that there was no justice anywhere. I am glad that no one told me then that my older sister, Sheyna, often fainted from hunger in school.

This is the way food functions in our lives; as sensuous sign it leads, through a winding trail of association, back into childhood, into hidden struggles and conflicts and that vast store of childhood knowledge tucked away from conscious awareness.

And yet we know that for the woman with an eating obsession food never quite yields its full evocative power. The bag of oranges we peel and stuff down practically without chewing, and without the simultaneous work of searching out the memory the food evokes, never manages to inform our struggle. Our food—this food of obsession that torments our lives—is used instead to swallow the memory for which it stands.

And so the work begins; this immense, arduous task of converting the hunger for food into knowledge of all those ancient relations and struggles and lost raptures of childhood.

Close your eyes, I say to women who sit opposite me in my consultation room. Can you remember the kitchen in the house where you lived when you were a child?

Women of all ages, women who have not been able to remember their childhood, women who have, as they tell me, not cried for many years, sit with their eyes closed describing the plastic cloth on the kitchen table, the bright color of the knobs on the cabinets in a room they have not seen since they were three or four years old. They see their mother young again or for the first time acknowledge an absent mother or recall a mother whose back was always turned, bent over the hot stove, ignoring them.

"I remember coming home from school in the afternoon. I see the back door and the empty kitchen. I call out for my mother. I slam the door. She always told me not to slam it. I walk into the room."

Here, she opens her eyes and shakes her head. "That's all I want to remember today." She is a woman in her late forties, a large, majestic presence, filling the room with her bright colors and her jewelry and her expensive clothes. She is a gourmet cook. A bon vivant, a superb raconteur. She was named Violet after her mother, but she calls herself Katrina, the name of her great aunt. For weeks she has regaled and entertained me, making evident to me the qualities that have won her renown as a society hostess. Very poor as a child, she has devoted years of her life to the organizing and presenting of fashionable banquets on behalf of charities that serve orphanages, homes for unmarried teenage mothers, the public wards of children's hospitals. After the guests have gone, as the maids are clearing the tables, she stands by herself in the kitchen hunched over the trays of food, devouring it.

Today she remembers her childhood for the first time in over thirty years. She closes her eyes again, and her face puckers with anxiety. "I remember the empty refrigerator. I was always hungry when I came home from school. I remember the moldy half of a grapefruit. A brown, wilted head of lettuce. There was nothing to eat. It scared me."

"Where was your mother?"

"I don't know. The kitchen is empty."

"Who got dinner for you?"

"I don't remember dinner."

"Try to recall. What else was there in the kitchen?"

"We had a drawer for bread. Lined with some kind of metal. There was a piece of dried bread with green spots on it." She hesitates, shaking her head again. And then, speaking very slowly, in a tiny voice, she describes an occasion when she went upstairs calling out for her mother. She remembers falling silent at the top of the stairs and tiptoeing down the hall. She remembers the anxious hunger, the feeling that she could starve to death. The cold house. The dust on the carpet outside her mother's room. She speaks as one who is in a trance, but her breast is heaving. And now, there comes before her, following her from the memory of the empty kitchen with its moldering food, the sight of her mother sitting slumped in the bathtub with a glass in her hand. "There was no one to feed me," she cries out in a husky voice of horrified recognition. "There was no one to feed me . . ."

The Primal Feast

Over the following weeks we go back to the kitchen again and again. The memory fills itself out, childhood rushes in and transpires there, all over again. For these were the scenes she did not wish to recall—the typical encounters of childhood, its formative engagements and climactic moments, and all of it there, fretful and turbulent behind the entertaining stories, the well-turned phrases. The father's grim silence when he came home from his trips away as a salesman. The shouting she could never get away from. She hid under the kitchen table, behind the stained plastic cloth. She sees again the neat row of bottles against the wall under the table. She remembers the hunger, the cold, the terror, the urgency, the need for food and for warmth and for a mother. She says, one day, that she believes her obsession with food must have something to do with that empty kitchen. This time she does not try to fight her tears. She says, some weeks later, that she learned to fend for herself because of that empty kitchen. As a child she figured out, she tells me, that if she went to play with a friend after school and hung around long enough the friend's mother would invite her to have dinner. She found out that anything was better than poverty and drunkenness and empty rooms. "I have spent my whole life," she says, "making sure the kitchen was never empty. I have married and stayed married in order to make sure my kitchen would be plentifully provided. I have used every ounce of capacity I have planning and serving meals in order to overcome this terrible fear of emotional starvation."

There is rage, left out of conscious awareness, driven out of memory, locked behind implacable doors. Rage another woman, named Dorothea, claims never to feel, never to have known. And yet, during the last three or four years, since her children have grown and she has gone "back to the world" as a volunteer in the campaign office of a local radical party, she finds that she has developed an "inexplicable dissatisfaction" with her body, that she is "thrown back and forth between bouts of greed and weeks of penance," her eating and her compulsive starvation both "fueled by a mean-eyed urge" that leaves her no rest. "I broke with my mother when I was thirteen years old. Since then, I have never looked back, never really spoken to her again, apart from exchanging superficial news about the boys and Samuel and work. It wasn't that I was angry at her. I just came to the conclusion we had to go our own ways. That she'd never like or understand me."

"You were never angry at her?"

"We never had anything to do with one another at all."

And so we make our way back into the kitchen. It is a large room in a country house, forgotten until now, where her family had lived when she was seven or eight years old. She sees a large, old pine table with a small drawer on the side. She smells cabbage. She likes the smell. She has been running through the kitchen, from the living room into her bedroom on the other side. She has been chasing the dog, hollering out at him with a loud, boisterous voice. Now she sees that her mother is in the kitchen, at the stove. But she keeps her back turned to her. Even when she yells very loudly the mother doesn't look over at her. She stands there, stirring something, shaking the pan, reaching up to the shelf above the stove, wiping her hands on her apron. The girl runs back through the room, and now she races out the kitchen door into the garden. It is cold. There is snow on the ground. She is barefoot. She plunges into the snow, shrieking and shouting, bounding after the dog. The smell of meat and cabbage comes outside with her. She is making a snowball. She is tossing it against a tree. She makes another and flings it back over her shoulder. She hears the crash of glass and turns, instantly frightened. She sees her mother's face. And now the mother is coming after her; the white apron with the grease stains looms up against the doorway. She is tossing the snowball into the air. She sees it sailing away from her, a spinning white luminous charge. Her mother is crying out, covering her face, and she is racing past her mother, into the kitchen, up to the stove, tugging at the heavy iron pot of soup, and it is spilling and her mother is coming after her and she had never remembered this kitchen or its rage. She had never recalled this violence of childhood, her struggle for the mother's attention won in childhood only through acts of transgression and rebellion. The rage comes back to her, as she sits opposite me in the room. This old rage of the neglected child. And she wonders, as the weeks pass and the first flush of the ancient anger passes, whether her many affairs, her broken marriages, her refusal to take the bar exam and complete her training as a lawyer, and the fat body ("which looks exactly like my mother's") which serves her as an excuse to hide herself in menial work, have something to do with this fury at the mother whose back was always turned as she stood bent over the stove and whom she left behind, she always believed, at the age of thirteen, without ever looking back.

We know that it is not easy—this hesitation in the face of a powerful desire to discharge tension by turning to food. One would prefer to eat and vomit, fast and eat again, and plan new diets and come up with new nutritional schemes for managing life's complexity. One would rather almost anything than face directly the awesome difficulty of becoming one's self. But women are in fact capable of the heroism that is required to strip away symptoms and face the self—in all its urgency, filled with needs the mother could not satisfy, confronting us with a terrifying sense of frustration that seems to condemn the mother as a failure, claiming us with its stern, authentic appetites that ask a far more complicated filling than food can provide. We are capable of the courage to face directly, and not through the counting of calories and weighing of pounds, the guilt and turmoil of the mother-separation struggle.

VI

THE FIRST TIME I tried deliberately to hesitate before I ate I found that I was scarcely able to drag myself off into my study to grab a pen. The urgency I felt, the pressure of the unknown force, made my hands shake. I wanted to move and act and eat and swallow. I wanted cookies and chocolate and gobs of peanut butter. How could I sit down at my desk, how could I hold back the frenzied rush, how could I think? I slashed out at the paper, scribbling frantic words, trying to understand my hunger. "Stillness," "Silence," "Quiet." That was as far as I got. I tossed the paper aside and moved quickly into the kitchen. My hand on the cupboard, I hesitated briefly; but in that split instant I felt the longing and it was not for food. I ate: chocolate, cookies, gobs of peanut butter. Unthinking now, I opened packages, pushing the food toward my mouth. And yet, the longing continued to make itself felt. It was larger even than food, a hunger bigger even than appetite. I never before, so far as I knew, had met this longing as a pure desire. I sat down finally, stuffed and sated, and watched this longing continue to rise. Something about it terrified me. I could not sit there with it for more than a moment or two. My stomach aching, my mouth puckered with the excess of sweetness, I went back to the cupboard and again I ate. Anything now. Spoonfuls of honey and jam. A broken crust of doughnut wrapped up in a ripped piece of cellophane paper. Anything to still this longing, to drive it away, to stuff it down and swallow it whole and annihilate it.

It took me weeks, perhaps months, before I could follow this longing for more than a few instants. Always, sooner or later, it compelled me to eat. I kept trying and failing. But meanwhile the pile of papers on my desk continued to grow. There were more words now: "Joy." "Ecstasy." "Intensity." This is what I was longing for? Some extreme sensation, either of peace or of intense rapture? This is what I was asking from food?

I remember the day I first broke through into my childhood. It was a flash of memory, fading almost as soon as it arose. But it showed me a little girl with a bag of cherries sitting on a bench in the Bronx park. She was swinging her legs, laughing and spitting the pits over her shoulder into the bushes. For some reason the sight of this happy child made me want to weep and drive her away. But this time, instead of trying to eat this little one into oblivion, I went over to my desk and wrote down the image: girl with cherries in the park. And now I put my head down on the desk and wept in earnest. The tears seemed to fill me; they had, apparently, a remarkable capacity to answer hunger. Now, when the longing rose up again, fierce and potent and undeniable, I saw that it reached for the wild joy, the unrestrained laughter of the girl on the park bench. I felt again the heat of that day, the trickle of sweat down the back of my legs. Joy. Ecstasy. The life force suddenly ripped free of restraint. Intense sensation. The rapture of life as it was visited that day, so long ago, on the small girl with tight braids and a little faded blue dress who ate her cherries and swung her legs and called out, I now remembered, in a husky voice to tell her older sister that she knew what the birds were saying when they sang.

The Primal Feast

Sometime later that same day, or perhaps on the next day, I remembered the way years and years before my mother had taken the cherries from the refrigerator and put them into a small bag for me and my sister. I could actually recall the taste of the dark, sweet fruit, which I had never eaten before. I saw the handle of the refrigerator, too high to reach. I saw my mother, bending over to take my hand. I saw her dark, serious face, softer than I ever remember seeing it. Was this my mother? I had always remembered us in conflict, struggling against one another in our pitched battle of opposing wills. And were there also, between us, moments of tenderness like this? Moments of simple joy and communion through food? She put her hand on my head. "Open your mouth and close your eyes," she said. And now the miracle of new taste, the burst of astonishment, eyes flying open. "Spit out the pits," she said and put her hand beneath my chin to receive them.

We eat in order to regain the joy and intensity, the wild rapture, the wonder and awe that were our childhood. And yet when we reach for food we are inspired by an urgent ambivalence that attempts to drive away memory of the past in the same act that brings food before us in an effort to recall it.

In the dreamy quiet of the cookie dipped in tea we remember. In the urgent rush, devouring the package of cookies from the cupboard, we stuff down memory and swallow it whole. Food, with its marvelous conjuring power, has the capacity to serve as a partial substitute for the strength of feeling that tries to return to us through our hunger. That hunger for food which is our hunger for intense sensation, for the immediacy and vividness of life, and for the child's unqualified response to it. We are trying to take back into us, through food, that intensity of feeling we left behind us when we left childhood behind us, long ago. Food is the archive in which we have stored the record of ourselves as wholer, more vital beings.

Thus, Marcel Proust, inspired by the taste of a fluted cookie dipped in tea, set down what is perhaps the finest piece of prose narrative written in French in the twentieth century. Dreaming, smelling, sipping, recollecting—Combray and childhood are restored to him, and Swann who fell in love with the prostitute Odette, and his parents' garden and fruit trees in flower:

And so it is with our own past. It is a labour in vain to attempt to recapture it: all the efforts of our intellect must prove futile. The past is hidden somewhere outside the realm, beyond the reach of intellect, in some material object (in the sensation which that material object will give us) which we do not suspect. And as for that object, it depends on chance whether we come upon it or not before we ourselves must die.

The past is hidden in the sensation derived from a material object. In the flavor of Madeleines dipped in lime-flower tea, which his aunt gave him to taste as a child, there has been stored the recollection of his childhood in Combray, where his aunt Leonie kept to her bed and where he would, on Sunday mornings, go to visit her. The years pass, he leaves childhood behind, he enters the world and forgets the past. And then one day he dips in a cup of tea that childhood cookie of potential recollection and is invaded by an exquisite pleasure that restores to him "the old grey house upon the street, where her room was," and there rises into conscious memory, "like the scenery of a theatre . . . the little pavilion, opening onto the garden."

So, too, a woman with an eating obsession is searching for the memory of things past. For in that past and in its hidden, troubled memory is the possibility of liberation from the unseen conflicts and ambivalence that keep her from moving into her own development and from the re-creation of herself she urgently requires. In that childhood she cannot bear to recall there is the rage she must find again and restore to herself so that she may redirect it against present tyrannies, of slenderness and contempt for women and doubt of her capacities and suspicion of her powers. In those ancient scenes of turmoil and struggle with the mother is the power also for her struggle to enter the future. The joy she needs is there, too, and the love and tenderness she once felt for this woman, her mother, who gave her life and struggled to nurture her. This same love and tenderness she needs to feel also for herself, a woman in struggle, as was her mother before her.

Women remembering childhood, by unraveling the hunger knot that binds them to food, restore the lost intensity of feeling known to the child. Gradually, over the months and years of this work they become capable of a keen and vivid sense of life's potential. They reclaim the child's expressive power, its playfulness, spontaneous creativity, love for learning, hunger for knowledge, and appetite for growth, these lost capacities that drive us to food in the vain hope that eating will fill the aching emptiness we feel when we live in alienation from our childhood and its powers. Gradually, in this labor of reclamation, our attachment to food as obsession is frayed and finally severed.

"There was the smell of vanilla and honey," a woman says. "I'll never forget it. She was like a fat, round cake herself, and I stirred and stirred and she said to me, 'Fifty times and not one over, that is how a cake is baked.' But I stirred fifty-one times. It wasn't to spite her. I wanted to do it my own way."

At the heart of a disordered relation to food there is a disorder in memory, a severe inner distance from those recollections that would require us to feel.

"And this is what I told to my daughter. You learn the rules of cooking and baking so that you can transcend them. And when she made a mess, and when she put twelve eggs into the batter and when she used up all the butter we had for dinner, did I yell at her? I took her in my lap (and believe me, I was angry), I rocked her, and I rolled my eyes over her head."

"The smell of onions cooking in chicken fat. I remember Mama. I remember the way she would get off the bus on her way home from work. Even in the coldest weather, and then she had to walk all the way home. But she brought us the biggest apples you've ever seen. That way we could afford them."

Women troubled in their relationship to food are troubled by an inability to summon and reexperience their childhood.

"I remember the time she let me make a whole meal by myself. Dad said I was already a better cook than Mom, and after that I never tried to cook again."

"She taught me arithmetic with a measuring cup. She taught me about pints and quarts and gallons and ounces. And I could add and subtract and even multiply when I was still in kindergarten."

At the heart of a disordered relation to food there is a need to draw back out of the past the child's enthusiasm for self-development.

"Her cake won the prize at the P.T.A. My mother's cake. All the girls got to taste it. It was the first time I saw a look of pride on her face. And I thought, I wanna grow up to be just like my mother."

"I threw it away, every single day at school. I threw away the lunch she made for me. I was ashamed of it. She used to give me immigrant food. I was ashamed of her, ashamed of my mother. But today, I think about that little bag of food. I remember. And we were poor, believe me, and I could just weep to think of how she was giving me herself like that, and I hid it under my coat and when lunchtime came I just threw it away."

"She used to wheel me through the park in my carriage. I remember . . . I was, how old? I would sit there in my knit cap with a Fig Newton in my fist. I saw the trees over my head. They had the new pale green of the first spring I ever saw, and ever since then, looking at them again each year, I think they taste like cookies and I remember my mother.''

"Blue water and yellow ships; the rusty glimmer of firelight; the fresh taste of bread and milk in her mouth; the sound of her mother's playing, which rippled on and on until it was shattered at last by a scream. . . .''

"We would come in from school, Mama was baking, she made zudhartkes (little cinnamon twists), the bread was ready, cooling on the table, but the zudhartkes she would take right out of the oven. She'd say, 'Careful, children. They're still hot.' And we smiled at each other because now Mama was back in control.''

"Then my dear mamma boiled water from the little brook, the most sparkling water I have ever seen, and when it just began to bubble she poured it over the tea, and then we drank. And, my dears, I never, *never* have such tea tasted!''

PART FOUR

Rites of Passage

I

There is silence at the table. Silence, as the older woman sets down the bowl of lamb stew simmered in red wine, the carrots and pearl onions cooked separately, stirred in at the last moment. She nods to her husband, assuring him that she has prepared a traditional family meal. She covers the dish of potatoes to keep them warm, brings out a basket of rolls wrapped in a flowered napkin, lifts the cover from the butter dish, fills the glasses with water, and raises her voice. She is calling to her daughter, asking her to come downstairs to join them for the meal. But her voice, which should have carried to the second floor, past the locked door, past the young woman's angry refusal to share this meal, cracks and hesitates. Her shoulders rise and fall; she raises her eyebrows, glancing at this angry man, who insists the girl come down to take her meals with them. She takes a step toward the stairs, trying again. "Daddy wants you to join us. It's Sunday . . ." But her voice lacks all conviction.

All this has a history. The last time the daughter attempted to eat this meal at the family table, chewing every mouthful thirty-five times, her father threw his napkin down on the table, rose up to his full height, grabbed her plate of vegetables, and pushed them down to the end of the table. He picked up his plate of meat and potatoes and shoved it toward her. He picked up his fork and held it up in front of her face. "You hear me?" he shouted. "From now on you'll eat what your mother puts on the table. You'll chew like a normal person. That's the last time you sit here like a cadaver chewing your cud. You want to be a member of this family, you'll eat what we eat."

Since then, five days of silence have gone by—that stubborn silence at the family meals, the girl pushing the food around in her plate, cutting up the meat into small and then smaller pieces, not really even trying to pretend she was eating. But today she has gone back to the steamed organic vegetables, the squares of tofu in their bowls of water, the jars of vitamins in the special cupboard she has prepared for herself, scrubbing out the pantry with an "ecologically sound" detergent, lining the shelves with rice paper and filling it with packages of dried sea-weed and fermented soy-bean. And now, alone in her room, she is violating the invariable custom of the shared Sunday meal.

This daughter, who will not come down to join them for the family meal, has been in the kitchen for the last hour or two, cooking a dish of steamed vegetables, mashing tofu, mixing it with soy sauce, and squeezing herself a large glass of fresh carrot juice.

The girl knows her mother is knocking. But she will not listen to entreaties. She will not pity the older woman, caught between them, trying to placate both of them. She sits there, chewing her food thirty-five times each bite. She will not come down to join them. She will never eat with HIM again. She will not eat meat and potatoes. She will not eat French bread with butter and garlic. She will eat her steamed vegetables and her tofu and her carrot juice, and if he forces her she will not eat anything at all.

She hears her father come upstairs. He is rattling the

handle. "Didn't I tell you not to lock your door? Open it, or I'll break it down," he is shouting. "Victor, Victor," her mother is urging. And then, in the same urgent, placating voice: "Just come sit with us," she is saying to her daughter. "We know you've already had dinner. I told Daddy you already ate."

The daughter has gone into her closet. She has closed the door and sat down on the floor. Next year, she is promising herself, she is not going to come home at all for summer vacation. She picks up an extra blanket from the closet shelf and puts it over her head. She does not want to think how it will all end. She does not want her father to yell at her mother. She does not want her mother to weep. Later, she'll go down, when her mother is washing dishes. She'll apologize. She'll try to explain to her. But she knows she won't be able to explain. "Look," she'll say: "Look, I just want to eat what I want to eat. I just want to do things my way. Why can't he let me?" And her mother, frowning, shaking her head, dropping her voice to a whisper: "But couldn't you try? Just for my sake? Just for a few weeks?"

And so, in yet another way, food and hunger become a guide. We have seen the way our hunger, having served to express a profound crisis in identity for a generation of women, opened down into the hidden guilt of the daughter about to surpass her mother's life. Food and hunger, troubling us as obsession, nevertheless have carried us back into childhood where we have been able to follow the pathway of identity formation and probe the earliest mother/daughter bond. Perhaps by now it is to be expected that food would serve us in the next inevitable movement that completes the cycle and carries us back out into culture and the generational dimension once again.

For the girl locking herself in the bedroom in order to eat the way she wants to eat is claiming the right to have a world view in common with her generation. Eat meat and potatoes, her father says to her. Eat the way we eat. That is how you will establish your right to be a member of this family. And she answers, closing her mouth against the food he pushes into her face: No, I will eat vegetables, I will have my own way of being in the world.

Initially she herself may not have experienced this connection between the food she eats and the world view she has espoused. But years later, when asked to talk about these foods and to look for meaning in this crisis of her late adolescence, she suddenly, and for the first time, delivers herself of an impassioned discourse upon the state of the world.

Looking at her across the room from me, I can see the astonishment softening the severe cast of her features, making her, a woman of thirty-two, look almost as young as the adolescent girl in this memory she is recounting. It is the moment we have been waiting for—that sudden emergence of the crucial scene from the past. Will we find here the line of meaning that runs between that moment fifteen years ago and the woman's behavior today?

Is it possible that her bean sprouts and tofu, her careful preparation of a solitary meal, her preoccupation with vitamins and minerals and the correct, organic way food is grown still stand for a cluster of preoccupations and concerns she knows to be in conflict with her father's traditional orientation and which she still cannot bring herself to express directly? Last year, at the age of thirty-one, she moved out of her family's home for the first time. And now, practically whispering, she spreads her hands in front of her and works it out carefully, point for point. Her refusal to eat meat allows her to express her concern with the way animals are treated in this culture. (She presses her pinky against her palm.) Her insistence upon organic vegetables is part of her preoccupation with the poisoning of the environment, the violence our culture shows toward nature, our disregard for the integrity of other forms of life. (Another finger pressed to the palm.) And now (her voice growing louder) she remembers an occasion when she first attempted to discuss these issues with her family. She remembers her mother's worried frown, the tightening of her lips, the little tap on her leg beneath the table, as the older woman attempted to caution her away from a topic that would create family discord.

And so, on that occasion, she did not or could not choose to alarm her mother or alienate her father, could not bring herself to separate from her mother's conciliatory mode of behavior, stopped herself in midsentence, as she says, and ''swallowed'' the words she was about to speak. She fell silent, did not bring up the issue again, and some weeks or a month later began to refuse meat, frown at the ''pallid vegetables'' on the table and took to shopping for her own food at the only market in her small town that carried organic vegetables, although she had to drive all the way across town to purchase them.

These vegetables she eats, chewing them carefully and with a ''reverent attitude,'' have acquired symbolic meaning for her, and she defends her right to them with a vigor and passion that seem puzzling even to herself. For now, if she gives in, even on one occasion, to her mother's persuasions to go back to the customary family meals, she is in danger of losing the only way she knows of expressing her own desire to be a unique and distinctive human being with a world view that unites her to her generation and separates her from the family ethos. For this girl eating alone in her room, food and her attitude toward food had become urgent and overpowering because they were an attempt to provide herself with a rite of passage into society and the next stage of her development.

''It has often been said,'' writes Mircea Eliade in *Rites and*

Symbols of Initiation, "that one of the characteristics of the modern world is the disappearance of any meaningful rites of initiation. Of primary importance in traditional societies, in the modern Western world significant initiation is practically nonexistent."

The purpose of a rite of passage in a premodern society is to move the individual from an earlier phase in the life cycle, to separate her from childhood and make possible the movement into the next stages of her own development. "The novice emerges from his ordeal endowed with a totally different being from that which he possessed before his initiation; he has become another." But the initiation ceremony must also awaken the individual to a sense of social and collective responsibility. "In modern terms we could say that initiation puts an end to the natural man and introduces the novice to culture." Thus, a rite of passage in tribal society accomplishes two fundamental purposes: the transformation of identity and the entry into culture.

As it happens, these two goals of a rite of passage are also the principal requirements of women today, as they move out of an earlier form of social and personal identity and seek their entry into culture. It seems inevitable that a generation undertaking this immense step and lacking every sort of ceremonial help with this movement would have to evolve a rite of passage for itself. If the society cannot provide it in a meaningful collective form, some kind of obsession may be necessary to bring at least to partial expression the turmoil and urgency we are feeling.

It must initially seem a great interpretive leap to claim that an obsession with food is an attempt to provide a ceremonial form by which women can enter culture. The idea of a "puberty rite," if the words are familiar to us at all, calls up a hazy impression of strange and primitive doings—dancing late into the night in an isolated camp in the bush; wizards climbing trees anointed with human blood, chanting as the initiates are led along into the clearing where they will remain in isolation from the rest of the tribe during the weeks of their ordeal. Indeed, the little we know of girls' initiation ceremonies can only intensify this impression of something remote and alien to modern life—the isolation in a small cabin from the time the menstrual blood first descends, the ritual baths, the girl painted with ocher, the tattooing, the blackening of the teeth.

Indeed, the overt expression of this ceremonial separation from childhood for the purpose of being initiated into collective life will necessarily differ in modern and earlier times. And yet it is possible to detect a significant ceremonial intention in the behavior contemporary women direct toward food. Nor should this surprise us. For a woman, of any age, coming of age in the sense I am using the words—to describe the movement into a new type of female identity—must manage to win a right of passage for herself into a society that has never before welcomed women. And she must, simultaneously, be brought back into old, forgotten forms of female knowledge and power, which it is difficult for her to reclaim since she associates so many of them with the oppression of her mother. Both these enterprises are in fact extremely radical activities, in their potential to challenge and transform traditional patriarchal culture. We would hardly expect that society itself would offer this rite of passage to women, who require it for the purpose of transforming the most fundamental norms of female identity. But we might well expect women, as a result of this cultural lack, to evolve some fragmentary and incomplete form of this rite of passage. Much of the obsessive quality of an eating disorder arises precisely from the fact that food is being asked to serve a transformative function it cannot carry by itself, although in earlier, tribal cultures food was always an essential part of those transformative, collective ceremonies through which individuals were brought, step by step, to separate from one phase of their development and enter the collective.

Indeed, in the various initiation rites Eliade describes, dietary restrictions and taboos are so universally apparent, along with a shared, tribal sense of the mythological significance of food, that we may be justified in claiming that an obsession with food is always, at heart, an expression of some attempt to bring about either profound personal transformation or an entry into collective life and its spiritual meanings.

II

THERE ARE, OF COURSE, significant differences between our food obsessions and the deliberate, fully evolved ceremonies of earlier cultures. In our time, for instance, a "tribal initiation" rite is required not only during adolescence (the age at which eating disorders typically develop) but for any woman who is attempting to enter society and to transform her own personality so that this movement may become possible. Indeed, when eating disorders begin to trouble the lives of women in all age groups, it is a sign that we are in urgent need of a ceremonial form to guide us beyond what may well be the collective childhood of female identity into a new maturity of female social development.

For a rite of passage does more than move the individual from one stage in the life cycle into a new relationship to culture. It also provides a highly elaborate, ritual enactment of the stresses and tensions and conflicts that accompany any such formidable transition. The collective ceremony, with its ordeals and highly formalized practices, brings to expression all the basic psychological needs of the individual who has entered the initiation. Thus, it is fascinating to discover that the basic "puberty rite" all over the premodern world consisted of an initial separation from the mother, which, as we have seen, is also the fundamental preoccupation and requirement of a woman with an eating disorder.

For girls, as Eliade writes, initiation begins with the appearance of the first menstrual blood. For "this physiological symptom, the sign of sexual maturity, compels a break—the young girl's removal from her familiar world. She is immediately isolated, separated from the community—which reminds us of the boy's separation from his mother and segregation. In either sex, then, initiation begins with a break, a rupture."

Thus, we may say that the contemporary woman, obsessed with food and using it as a symbolic expression of her mother-separation struggle, is in fact attempting to enact a rite of transformation, which, however, remains split off from its collective significance. The collective ceremonies of tribal people made it possible for young people to enter and intensify and finally to leave behind the obsessions and preoccupations that must inevitably arise during the violent upheaval of a major developmental step. They did this by subjecting the initiate to a variety of ordeals, all of which had a basic symbolic and transformative function, and by surrounding the initiate with the support, wisdom, and participation of the tribe. The inevitable need to separate from the mother in order to get on with the next stages of development is given ceremonial acknowledgment and is then woven into the overall needs and purposes of the collective. Consequently, these ceremonies, with their profound understanding of human necessity, also lay great stress upon the creation of a sacred ground, where the initiation and its enactments might take place.

The sacred ground provides for a place apart, in which the initiate is physically isolated from the daily life of the rest of the tribe and symbolically separated from the conditions of her earlier life, from the mother, and from her childhood. It is a ground where transformation can take place, precisely because the need for it has been recognized as essential. Here, alteration in the human personality is invited to occur and becomes possible because a formal expression is given to the underlying psychological tension and upheaval.

Indeed, the initiatory ordeals universally associated with rites of passage are an essential way of expressing both psychological urgency and transformative intentions. These ordeals vary, depending upon the tribe in which they are found. But common among them are requirements that the novices not "go to bed until late in the night," as well as prohibitions against eating and drinking. Frequently silence is imposed.

Eliade interprets these initiatory ordeals as an attempt, on the part of the tribe, to bring the initiate back to an infantile state. "Among the Ngarigo, for example, during the six months the novice spends in the bush his guardian feeds him, putting the food into his mouth. The inference would seem to be that the novice is regarded as a newborn infant and hence cannot feed himself without help. For . . . in some puberty ceremonies the novice is assimilated to a baby unable to use its hands or to talk." Within the tribal setting the meaning of this reassimilation to infancy becomes symbolically clear. For the initiate must die to the earlier stage in the life cycle, leave childhood behind, and so be reborn into the life of the collective.

Now as it happens all these features of a rite of passage are perceptible in the behavior of the girl who refuses to eat at the family table. Her behavior requires interpretation, of course, but her compulsions and obsessions, when subjected to a sustained, symbolic scrutiny, yield a meaning closely akin to that which exists in tribal cultures.

To begin, then, with the young woman who refused to join in the family meal: it is apparent that in her insistence upon the type of food she chooses and prepares for herself, she intends a clear statement of separation from the mother's traditional appeasements and conciliations. This lighter, vegetarian food, which the mother would also prefer but which she eats virtually in secret, at lunch alone with her child, becomes the daughter's emphatic means of differentiating herself from the mother's resigned loyalty to the father's life-style and values. For years, the father's meat and potatoes have represented the long continuity of generational values that he expects his wife to share and propogate. And now the daughter's "organic, new-age foods" become, in her mute rebellion, a means of moving away from the mother who dutifully, against her own inclination, prepares these foods and serves them up as a sign of her self-sacrifice and submission to the family norm. In the daughter's self-evolved rite of passage, food has become the principal expressive vocabulary; it separates her symbolically from the mother and isolates her physically from the principal gathering place of family cohesion. Its purchase, its preparation, and its consumption now serve to move her apart into that sacred ground where her separation from the family and her introduction to culture should then take place.

But the parallel between her behavior and the ceremonies of tribal people goes even further. For in her dedicated preparation of the special cabinet where she stores her food, she is, in fact, making a sacred ground for herself. This is apparent in the significance she herself attaches to this preparation—the special detergent she uses for cleaning the shelves, the rice paper she puts on and keeps clean and changes weekly; the methodical, obsessive ordering of the packages and boxes of her food supply. And the pictures of herbs and medicinal plants she hangs on the doors of her private cabinet—are they not highly reminiscent of those ritual symbols and sacred emblems staked out along the path to the sacred enclosure? Naturally, these elaborate preparations of a place apart draw the family's attention—the mother hovers nearby, watching this "bizarre behavior" with increasing alarm and consternation, as she attempts to keep Dad away from the pantry that had for years been used only to store newspapers and boxes and old boots. And he, refusing to remember that these things have been cleared out and stored in the basement, is continually going in there to find something he has misplaced. And so his daughter discovers him one day as he stands in perplexed rage, puffing out his cheeks and demanding that her "nonsense" be cleared away. The mother, delegated to instruct her daughter about the father's disapproval, puts on a martyred face when she and the girl are alone; she sighs deeply and raises her eyebrows in a mute appeal, which drives her daughter into yet more elaborate tending of her sacred ground.

Likewise, the health-food store at the edge of town has taken on for this girl the quality of a "place apart." She goes there even when she does not need food, reads through the magazines, talks with the woman behind the counter, thoroughly investigates all the pamphlets on vitamins and herbal cures, sips a glass of celery juice with watercress and garlic.

Inevitably, to be sure, her interest in "health" and "diet" and herbs and minerals and vitamins leads her to special "ordeals," as her father in fact conspicuously calls them. She chews slowly, each week taking longer and longer to swallow a single mouthful of food; soon, she eats only a meal a day, loses weight, begins to look gaunt and hollow. Now her slender body serves to separate her even further from her mother, who has always been "a bit overweight." And soon, for reasons she does not at all understand, she fasts one day a week and tries to stay awake for the entire night, during which she pores through her herbal cookbook with its elaborate classification of healing recipes. When she is forced to take her meals at the table, she sips her vegetable juice through a straw to keep herself from eating any of the family foods that may tempt her. And now we see the way this contemporary young woman has managed, in her suburban home, to create for herself the essential trappings of a ceremonial passage into what should be the next stages of her development. As the novice in the bush, who is not allowed to feed himself without help, who must not sleep or eat for days, who is required to drink by sucking through a reed, who must remain silent in obedience to tribal rite, she too has returned herself to the infantile condition, hoping for rebirth into the next stage of the life cycle.

She fails; tragically, indeed, given the intensity of her effort, the dedication and discipline she brings to it, and the urgency of the underlying transformative need she feels. As she withdraws gradually from social life in order to tend to her dietary prohibitions and restrictions, her food obsession begins to isolate rather than unite her to the collective transformative undertaking of her generation. She cannot move, she remains stuck in repetitive behavior. The rite of passage becomes blocked and stagnant. She pursues the repetitive round of an obsession, increasingly with each day trapped by its rigors—the long drive to the health-food store, the careful changing of the rice paper in her storage cabinet, the exact balancing of vegetables with grain for assuring their precise yield of minerals and vitamins. She fails to grasp the underlying transformative significance, although it comes just close enough to keep her bound to this behavior that promises a meaningful movement away from childhood and into culture. She is in need of a collective understanding, she must be able to place her preoccupation with food and diet within the context of her generation so that she can move on, past her loyalty to the sacred ground that has grown sterile with compulsive repetitiveness. She must get on with the task, move the struggle for identity and transformation forward, claim herself, find meaningful work, move into society, mature. Instead, she keeps expanding the ordeals, driving herself even further back into infancy as she grows silent and gradually refuses to eat all but the most minute amount of steamed food, hoping for a rebirth that cannot take place because she cannot get beyond these trappings of transformation and actually manage to leave the mother, separate from the family, claim the new identity with its full sense of collective responsibility.

Here, of course, we will have an immediate sense of an important difference between tribal practices and contemporary obsessions—for it is, in the tribal setting, the understanding of the religious meaning of the food that allows the dietary prohibitions to be gradually stripped away. "Dietary prohibitions also have a quite complex religious function . . . in some tribes dietary prohibitions are successively removed as myths, dances, and pantomimes teach the novice the religious origin of each kind of food." Consequently, we would expect that the failure to fathom this dimension of meaning in the food obsession of contemporary women would leave the dietary prohibitions in place, precisely because the obsession with food has been split off from its underlying ceremonial and transformative intention. And so the girl regresses to infancy but does not get reborn; she retreats to a place apart but cannot proceed back into the collective; she subjects herself to ordeals but does not strip them away through an understanding of their spiritual and mythic meaning. Separated from the mother through her slenderness and her stubborn refusal to eat the family's food, she is yet aligned to her by the failure of her development, her increasing dependency, her exclusive preoccupation with food as a means of expressing herself.

And now we see that, through the most tragic of ironies, she has narrowed her world to that very sphere of preoccupation that has defined her mother and provided, for years and years, her sole creative outlet. Like her mother, she too now is consumed by the purchase, preparation, and consumption of food.

She remains isolated in her father's home, split off from women her own age, for soon her obsessive care for the sacred cupboard makes it impossible for her to return to school. The rite has failed her; it has not provided passage into society and her own maturity, but instead has managed to exclude her from the culture she needs to enter as a being transformed. Her eating disorder has disordered but not altered her life. She is eighteen years old. She locks the door to her room. She reads the government pamphlet on trace minerals in foods and recites, beneath her breath, the healing potential of flowering plants. If she does not find help in uncovering the essential meaning of her behavior, its obsessions and compulsions will continue to proliferate and for the next fourteen years the door to her room will remain closed to that wider vista of female possibility she glimpsed so briefly as a member of her fateful generation.

III

THIS ATMOSPHERE OF A rite of passage, apparent in the behavior of the girl with the sacred cupboard, is perhaps even more evident in the lives of college women afflicted with food obsessions. Certainly, the setting of a university provides a rather obvious form of "sacred ground." The women are isolated from their families and from their mothers, set apart in a clear way from their childhood conditions and invited, through this movement into collective, intellectual life, to prepare themselves for an entry into culture. Where the universities fail to offer other features of tribal initiation, the extracurricular social life on campus makes good the lack. Sororities provide the mock-mythical form of those ordeals with which we have become familiar in the tribal setting; late nights become a regular feature of campus social life, as do the dances that frequently last until early hours of the morning, evoking those collective dances that in tribal cultures frequently bring initiation ceremonies to an end. The posters and photographs that adorn a woman's room easily take on the significance of sacred images. And there are of course those elaborate ceremonies of bathing and preparing the hair, make-up, and self-adornment that mirror the face-painting and ritual bathing customary in the rite of passage. But it is, of course, the dietary taboos and prohibitions contemporary college women bring about for themselves in their obsessions with food that form the most conspicuous parallel to the rites and customs of tribal initiation.

The most casual observer of college life today may easily detect the "special atmosphere" of women's food behavior. The bottles of diet dressing the older girls carry into the dining rooms line the tables at every meal and soon instruct the younger women in this dieting obsession that has become an essential feature of college life. The women regularly avoid the food lines serving meat and carbohydrates, but flock around the salad bar, where few men are ever found. Conversation among women, as they readily admit, is focused primarily on discussions of calories and losing weight, the women eagerly confiding to one another, in rather hushed, reverent tones, discoveries and secrets about new diets.

This behavior, with its dietary prohibitions, its female bonding, its exclusion of the opposite sex, its instruction of younger by older women, its cultic atmosphere of whispered preoccupations, has the serious intention to make ceremony out of daily life and to restore to the mundane surface of the contemporary world the collective depth of the tribal experience of female initiation. There, too, in that more ancient ritual, the boys are excluded. The girls are grouped together and are initiated by older women into women's secrets. And "naturally," as Eliade says, "there are some dietary restrictions almost everywhere."

These correspondences must, of course, be taken broadly; it is not a question of precise detail, but a common shading and atmosphere that allow us to sense the underlying intention of an eating obsession. Thus, when I read in *Ms.* that "at least half the women on campus today suffer from some form of eating disorder," I am inclined to detect in this statement an invitation to look for collective ceremonial meanings. For it should be clear by now that in the absence of meaningful ceremonies of passage, women will be driven to evolve compulsive and obsessive equivalents to these ancient social rites—and for the same purpose, precisely, of guiding themselves through the developmental transition so that they can move into culture.

The effort toward this collective transformation is apparent even in the most self-destructive and seemingly bizarre rituals and ordeals the women bring about for themselves during their first years of separation from the family. Equally apparent is the tendency to hand down from older to younger woman this new form of tribal lore. "Jan had never had a weight or eating problem before entering college, but she slowly began to put on weight her first year at a large Midwestern university, where she lived on campus in a dorm. Jan went on a diet, lots of exercise and skipping meals—and dropped 15 pounds. Then the weight crept back on, the comments started from her mother, her sisters, and her boyfriend, and Jan began to binge regularly every time she was criticized about her weight. At a family picnic the summer before her junior year, 'my cousin, who was anorexic, gave me the idea to vomit. She had learned it from her roommate, who'd heard it from her sister.' "

Interestingly enough, this new cult behavior she had learned from her cousin, who had learned it from her roommate, who had learned it from her sister, made Jan extremely eager to leave the family and get back to the university, where she could pursue her initiation into her generation's collective, ceremonial forms without her mother's intervention. She wanted, in short, to return to the sacred ground of obsession her generation has carved out for itself in its efforts to extend its social identity. "Once she'd learned about vomiting, Jan was eager to return to school where she could binge and vomit without her mother nosing around. She knew it was wrong, but thought it was a great way to be able to eat what she wanted. Ultimately, Jan's bingeing and vomiting severely disrupted her life."

Evidently the need for some form of social ceremonial is sufficiently urgent to compel women of the present generation to transform even the most shameful, private compulsions into collective forms. Thus, self-induced vomiting, which some years ago was rarely confided even to a therapist, today has become a group activity from which the atmosphere of shameful secrecy has begun to be removed.

"Renee, now a senior at the University of Arizona, says that she and other sorority members are open about their bulimic behavior, especially if they're bored. 'We go out together and spend thirty dollars on food, knowing all the time that we'll throw it up. If we're somewhere with only one bathroom we take turns throwing up, but if there are stalls we'll do it at the same time.'"

And so the hushed, private behavior becomes a collective social form, a distinctive form of female bonding, a public declaration of a generation's unique transformative goal.

"Another high-risk area of college life where bingeing and vomiting is peer-approved is competitive athletics. Karen Lee-Benner . . . clinical coordinator of UCLA's Eating Disorders Clinic, treated two world-class gymnasts for bulimia. She says that at least one of those patients told her that the entire gymnastics team would binge and vomit together following a meet—a purely social thing."

Ultimately, bingeing and vomiting will severely disrupt any woman's life; but initially they hold out the promise of collective initiation through those very ordeals and dietary restrictions that universally accompany such initiations throughout the tribal world. Vomiting, which in our culture seems bizarre, disgusting, and abhorrent, in fact has a long-standing cultic tradition, the very edge of which these young women seem to touch.

Andrew Weil, a graduate of Harvard Medical School, in his arresting book, *The Marriage of the Sun and the Moon,* describes the way vomiting is used in the training of students of highly developed religions.

> *Instructional materials on yoga urge students to learn to vomit voluntarily, to practice it regularly, and to perform it as a morning ritual, much as many people gargle. American Indians who eat hallucinogenic plants that cause nausea often vomit effortlessly and unself-consciously. Vomiting is even a central part of certain Indian rituals, such as the sahuaro wine festival of the Papagos, held near the summer solstice in the Sonoran Desert along the Mexico–United States border. The Papagos force themselves to drink as much as possible of a fresh wine made from the sweet, red fruit of giant cactuses. The vomiting and urinating that follow are supposed to help bring on the summer rains and thereby ensure survival through the hottest season.*

It is clear, of course, that vomiting in all these ritual forms has a spiritual application that remains absent from the behavior of contemporary women, who are trapped in an obsession with food and weight that frequently destroys their social adjustment and their lives. But it is equally evident that their entire obsession with food is a desperate effort to produce the atmosphere of initiation through which they might be born into the new phase of the life cycle and enter the collective thus transformed and fully aware of its mythic traditions. Everything is present except the sense of inner meaning: the removal to a sacred ground where initiation can take place; the separation from the mother and the conditions of childhood; the instruction by older women; the entry into distinctive forms of female bonding through the choice of special foods and the practice of special rituals, confided first as secrets and then engaged in as ceremonial social forms; dietary restrictions and taboos, physical ordeals of self-denial and overcoming, bizarre practices with symbolic meanings.

The difference in the atmosphere surrounding food a generation ago will be vividly apparent in this account of college life in 1927. It is M.F.K. Fisher again, sensitive as always to the culinary dimensions of existence. This time she and her cousin Nan are at a small college and it is serving terrible meals. Nevertheless, as she says: "We ate them ravenously, because classes were almost a two-mile walk from Hall, and by the time we had sprinted home for lunch we were hungry indeed. By the time we had walked back and then to the Hall again for dinner we were frankly starved, and would joyfully have wolfed down boiled sawdust."

It was, of course, that highly revealing word that first caught my attention. "Joyfully," she says. And I, reading this passage, shake my head in wonder. A woman wolfing food down joyfully? I read on, increasingly astonished by her description of Sunday breakfasts and hot cinnamon rolls.

"We had to eat them by a certain time . . . undoubtedly a dodge to get us up for church. Nan and her roommate Rachel and I used to dress in our church clothes, eat cinnamon rolls until we were almost sick, and then go back to bed." To be sure, by midafternoon the young women eating with such exuberant gluttony are "indigestibly awake" and end their day in "homesick mopes, misunderstandings, and headaches."

This is the food turmoil familiar a generation ago. The hearty eating, the wolfing down of cinnamon rolls, the staying in bed on a Sunday, the homesick blues have a definite relation to the experience of young women in college today. But the food behavior remains within manageable bounds, even when it carries emotional implications of loneliness and the stress of first separation from the family. This collegial gobbling of the 1920s stands always at the edge of humor, without either the extremity or the driven desperation evident in women's lives today, and without also that larger, ceremonial sense of the rite of passage.

"Quite often Rachel and Nan and I would invent some excuse . . . a birthday or a check from home or an examination passed . . . and would go to The Coffee and Waffle Shop, where we could have four waffles and unlimited coffee or a five-course meal for forty cents. Then we would go to the theatre and eat candy; there were still small companies playing *Smilin' Through* and *Seventh Heaven* then, or traveling magicians. And after the show we'd have another waffle, or two or three cups of hot chocolate."

There is no mention here of the fear of food, an obsession with slenderness, a terror of gaining weight; there is no evidence of laxatives or vomiting, no indication of special dietary taboos. There is the down-to-earth camaraderie of girls liberated from the mother's watchful eye and taking advantage of that freedom.

"Always for dessert there was pie and ice cream, on separate plates but to be eaten in alternating bites. Sometimes there were two kinds of pie, pumpkin and mince, with homemade eggnog ice cream, rich enough to make your teeth curl."

Food and youth and boys and girls and dates and eating. And no one seems ashamed of it. Boys and girls participate in it together, it remains a social not a cultic form of group expression. "On dates, which were limited because we were Freshmen, we drank chocolate or coffee and almost always ate chili beans. We would sit out in the cars, no matter how cold it was, and drink and eat. Then we would go back to the dance or the Hall. Everybody did that, and I suppose everybody smelled of chili powder and onions, so we never noticed it."

Clearly, these young girls were living in a generation in which the stress of female identity has not yet tightened around their lives, choking them off from the exuberance of youth, the giddiness, the silliness, the affirmation of life and the gluttony that goes along with it. "We would lock the door, and mix the cheese and anchovy together and open the ginger ale. Then we would toast ourselves solemnly in our toothbrush mugs, loosen the belts on our woolen bathrobes, and tear into that crisp cool delightful lettuce like three starved rabbits.

"Now and then one or another of us would get up, go to a window and open it, bare her little breasts to the cold sweep of air, and intone dramatically, 'pneu-mo-o-onia!' Then we would all burst into completely helpless giggles, until we had laughed enough to hold a little more lettuce. Yes, that was the best part of the year."

It is difficult to imagine a young woman of our time describing her experience of gluttony in these terms. For the woman today uses food not to celebrate life or youth or the capaciousness of adolescent appetite or even the small blues and manageable woes of freshman liberty. The food obsessions of contemporary women are a deadly serious affair precisely because of the imperative need for female transformation expressed through them, which we have failed to articulate sufficiently for the women of our time.

We have lost an innocence where food is concerned. And this fact tells us, as perhaps nothing else can, how important and urgent a generation we are in our frantic efforts to change the very idea of female nature. In the absence of more deliberate and intentional ritual forms for the transformation of ourselves, food has to provide a weighty emblematic service that leaves no space for innocent delights and healthy gluttony.

Indeed, the food obsessions of contemporary women provide yet a larger common ground with tribal initiation ceremonies than anything we have mentioned thus far. For contemporary women have a shared transformative goal they discuss obsessively among themselves, although, unlike women in the tribal setting, they remain profoundly unaware that they have engaged in their elaborate ordeals as part of an effort at personal and social transformation. In fact, however, whenever contemporary women make themselves vomit, it is because they are determined to become more slender than nature has intended women to be. And thus their obsession with slenderness marks their concern with "putting an end to the natural 'man' and introducing the novice to culture," which Eliade has described as the fundamental intention of an initiation rite.

The preoccupation with slenderness may be seen then as the only form women have found so far to express the complex transformative burden they carry as a generation. If a woman is not able to bring about other forms of personal and social transformation, she may yet express her urgent need for it by an obsessive attempt to transform her body, to remove it from nature and bring it gaunt and slender into culture.

"The only reason I want to stop is I'm afraid all the vomiting might affect my unborn children," says another college woman quoted in *Ms.* "Otherwise, I just want to be thin, whatever it takes."

We are now in a position to hear, in this extreme statement, an urgency about transformation the woman is unable to trace back to its authentic aim. If vomiting is the cult method of bringing about this transformation, then vomiting will be pursued at any risk and will, in the process, be converted into a negative, shadow ceremony of loyalty to this collective goal.

But here we come to another essential distinction between intentional ritual and ritualized obsession, which seems always to arise in the absence of appropriate collective forms. Intentional ritual, if we could elaborate it in an authentic and meaningful way, would serve to alleviate the self-destructive excess of the transformational experience by providing forms and measures for the passage from nature into culture. Women today, because they cannot bring their natural body into culture without shame and apology, are driven to attack and destroy that body. We have followed the tendency for this aggression against the female body in psychological terms, drawing it out from the original mother/child relationship. But now we must observe the way the cultural dislike for women and for the mature female body reinforces the rage against the body that has dogged our steps since childhood. Women today seem to be practicing genocide against themselves, waging a violent war against their female body precisely because there are no indications that the female body has been invited to enter culture. Where we require, after thousands of years of exclusion from culture, a ritual of entry and welcoming through which we could be reconciled with the female body and instructed in its mysteries and power, we are offered instead a sustained social coercion to reduce the body, to make it smaller than nature intended it to be and perhaps to destroy it altogether as we move out of the home and into the world.

Women respond to this pressure by a contradictory strategy of mastery and avoidance. Consequently, they are involved again in a significant shifting of the ground. We have seen this happen before now in this lengthy process of substitution that gradually builds the obsessive entrapment. We know how the struggle for identity expresses itself as a preoccupation with eating; we have seen the mother-separation struggle replaced by a concern with food. Now, we can observe the way a woman shifts her need for an entry into culture away from the radical transformation of her personality and focuses this transformative imperative upon her body.

It is at this moment that the full measure of her essential loneliness as a woman comes over her. Even in the act of vomiting with her friends she is alone in the confusion and despair she does not allow herself to express until her symptoms become so acute they force awareness on her. Here, at this urgent developmental moment, carrying a generation's transformational burden, she is abandoned by her mother, who cannot help her articulate her dilemma, and she is failed by her culture, which has not yet addressed itself to the enormous task presently confronting her.

And so she proliferates her concern with diet, ordeals, exercise, and poundage, hoping in vain to effect a more basic alteration of being, which, however, continues to elude her precisely because she does not engage the underlying tensions of separation and development a genuine rite of passage would help her to express. She thus stops short of the ultimate goal involved in a rite of passage. The fundamental existential movement never takes place. So long as she stays locked into this deadly game of self-starvation, enforced slenderness, or self-induced vomiting, she cannot become aware of her underlying guilts, her sense of profound disloyalty in separating from the mother, or her brooding, half-conscious sense that her culture, after opening the doors to its most highly prized institutions, does not really welcome female development after all.

This failure is, to be sure, the very essence of an obsession. It allows the woman to express an incomplete form of the basic desire for change, but in a sphere where the deeper, more significant psychological transformation she and her generation require is never actually engaged. And thus the obsession, which hides within it a potentially radical critique of women's role in culture and society, comes little by little to sabotage the struggle for a new and distinctive form of female being. For now, a woman's slender body, which serves to differentiate her from her mother and to transform her with regard to culture, is gradually worked over until, in this complex symbolic drama of failed transformation, yet another purpose emerges, which once again aligns the behavior of a contemporary woman with tribal preoccupations and cultic practices. For this slender body stripped of traditional female attributes is (as we have seen) soon brought as closely as possible into the condition of muscularity and leanness usually deemed appropriate for males.

This crossing-over of gender implicit in the physical image of the lean and muscular boyish woman is found also in tribal initiation rites. As Eliade observes: "Here we recognize the theme of the temporary androgynization and asexuality of novices. . . . For cases are known in which girls are dressed as men during their initiation period, just as boys wear female clothing during their novitiate."

We have already observed the tendency among contemporary women to dress themselves in male attire. But now we can deepen our understanding. If, on the one hand, women dress as men to evade responsibility for the new female identity, they may, simultaneously, make use of this male attire on their boyish-slender bodies as part of a ceremonial experimentation with qualities of assertion, mastery, and social authority we have always limited to men. Indeed, employed for this purpose, their behavior once again assimilates itself to an older stratum of cultural necessity and transforms even the advertising pages of a popular magazine into a cult object. Stretched out in a dramatic diagonal across one of the front pages of *New York* magazine, the recent Calvin Klein advertisement for women's jockey shorts will leave us in no doubt about the androgynization of the female body. Surely this near-nude form, with its lean muscularity, modest pelvic bulge, uplifted arms, the small breasts now virtually indistinguishable from well-developed pectoral muscles, can be taken, even with repeated scrutiny, as belonging equally to the male or female sex.

The eating disorder, the obsession with food and slenderness, the dressing in male attire that seems to accompany the food preoccupations of this generation open themselves to yet another interpretation. For now we see that this assumption of male qualities is a temporary part of women's struggle to evolve a new social identity in which women must, during their rite of transition, try out qualities and attributes the culture has long forbidden to women and assigned exclusively to men.

This sort of symbolic potential in the female body was used to the full in the film *Personal Best,* where the well-trained body of Mariel Hemingway brought into graphic expression a young woman's capacity for muscular self-assertion and athletic prowess. But this highly developed physique the actress acquired through great effort seems to have evolved a unique drama of its own, outside the fictional scope of the film itself. To prepare for the part of an Olympic pentathlete, the movie star for almost a year "trained four hours a day, swimming, bicycling and weight lifting to add 14 pounds of muscle to her 5'10" frame and cut her body fat in half." This new body made of the star a new type of female pin-up, instantly picked up by *Playboy* for its modish appeal. And there, in spite of its sponsor's undoubtedly exploitative intentions, it continued to resonate with those qualities of independence and self-determination that were characteristic of the film's heroine.

Undoubtedly, *Playboy* did not sense the radical implications of this new body image, but it seems to have disturbed the movie star herself, who has since given up weight lifting. "I don't want to be that big," she said last year. "That was an uncomfortable body for me."

The movie star, whose body has come to stand for the new, liberated woman, free enough to choose a woman as lover, tough enough to compete successfully for a place in that robust world of sports that once was a precinct reserved for males, grew so uncomfortable in her large, athletic body that she offered it up as sacrifice—literally, beneath the surgeon's knife.

In 1983, two years after her part in *Personal Best,* Mariel Hemingway underwent an operation to have her body changed. She emerged, in this horrifying reversal of the rite of passage, transformed back into the typical, stereotyped image of a sexy, voluptuous woman. Her breasts surgically enlarged, she can boast the 36-24-36 dimensions of the ideal female body of the 1950s. Now she can be featured in a new movie, this one of "flesh and graphic violence," a "walking, talking center fold, as clean-cut and passionless and about as deep as the paper on which her pictures are printed." She insists, meanwhile, that the movie "does not exploit her." *Playboy,* however, definitely will. And now this young star, whose athletic body provided a concrete image of the new female experimentation in social role, appears in ten pages of 1983's December issue of the magazine, standing for everything contemporary women are struggling not to be.

"She wasn't uncomfortable about her size when she was growing up," Mariel's mother tells *People* magazine. "I guess she did it for the part."

"I thought about it very carefully before I did it," the daughter says. "I decided I didn't want to go through life being looked on as just an athletic tomboy."

These questions of role and role reversal are so pressing that they continue to shape urgent, even tragic images of themselves in places where we would least expect them. And thus, on the cover of the issue of *People* magazine in which the story of the enlarged Mariel Hemingway is told are pictures of both Hemingway and Karen Carpenter. But how could language possibly do justice to all that this single page of a popular magazine thrusts before us here? These two images of female self-alteration speak in all their silent eloquence of the tragic failure of authentic transformation in women's lives: Hemingway in her new, seductive décolletage on the same page with the strained, stressed, gaunt, and emaciated Karen Carpenter, who also sacrificed her body and died of the effort to make it smaller and more slender than nature intended it to be. If these two images speak to us about our condition as women today, they would seem to deliver the covert warning that we had better do what Mariel Hemingway has done if we don't want to end up as Karen Carpenter.

Can we doubt now that there is sufficient urgency in this question of the new identity for women to shape these quasi-rites of passage? Can we doubt that in the absence of meaningful ceremonial forms we will make use of our bodies, our appetites, even our lives to bring this transformative imperative to expression?

But let us spell out clearly the problem in this enterprise of cross-gender experimentation. For Mariel Hemingway, unlike the pentathlete she portrayed, remained a pin-up, her muscular body representing qualities the woman herself evidently was not able as yet to achieve. And therefore we must wonder whether it was the uneasy tension between the empty image and the absent accomplishment that finally drove the star into that surgical intervention. For this is indeed the dilemma of the young woman of today—boyish, she is not, however, free to leave home without guilt and embark upon the paths of legitimate social identity; dressed in jeans with a zip-front fly, she plans a life-style in which the basic female right to autonomy and independence is never essentially engaged. Dressed in her jockey shorts, her androgynous body covers the page of a magazine as a sorry reminder of how easily our deepest, most essential struggle is taken from us and exploited and finally returned, reworked now into a hollow imagery that mocks our failure to achieve the substantive gains the image evokes.

An obsession hides, disguises, and ultimately betrays the transformation of personality it attempts to imitate. And therefore we would expect to find yet a further danger in this tragically self-defeating effort at change, whether it expresses itself through a preoccupation with losing weight or becomes manifest in the newer female fanaticism of the muscular body.

For, even if we should succeed in taking on through the donning of male shape and attire qualities that before now were the exclusive right of men, we still would not have the opportunity, within the obsession, to bring these new, formerly forbidden traits into some creative synthesis with the traditional values of female identity.

Ladies Home Journal of November 1981 speaks to this question. In an article called "Inner Beauty: Sexy New Lingerie for Every Body," women arrange themselves in postures and garments that aim to suggest the variety of life choices presently available to us. There is, of course, the traditional "sexy . . . sheer black teddy," which is considered "naughty but nice." Apparently, women in the 1980s are permitted, even in the pages of *Ladies Home Journal,* to have sexual identities. There is the older woman clothed in "executive grey" lingerie for wearing under her "tailored suits." There are to be sure the traditional "sweetly demure camisoles" that will help us in "brushing up on looking innocent," in case the sexy and professional opportunities at the top of the page should prove to be too alarming to us. And there are "tender" underclothes for the athlete and appropriate garments for the woman "rugged on the outside" who nevertheless wishes to remain "beguiling within."

Five styles of lingerie, five statements about the identity choices available to women in our culture today—and all of it in an effort to assure us that we can continue to wear the true and traditional female identity next to our skin, hidden beneath these new male clothes we put on to make our way into their world. For surely the covert message of all these bras and panties and slips is the reassurance that we can maintain the soft, seductive, innocent, enchanting, beguiling, tender qualities always associated with our sex, even now that we have begun to transform ourselves into men.

We need to get beyond these emblematic clothes conversations, to get in there and experiment directly with ways of carrying our sensuality into the world of our daytime endeavor. We need to move our sexuality beyond the coyness and passivity of our traditional role, so that the self-assertion and autonomy to which these male clothes invite us may become part also of the way we give and receive in love and desire. Perhaps, unthinkable as yet, some extraordinary combination of qualities is yet possible, some reorganization of what we call masculine or regard as female. A woman of authority rearing her children, setting those stern but compassionate limits a woman would be so good at, no longer abdicating responsibility by threatening the child with the paternal prohibitions Daddy will be bringing home with him after work. A woman handing down to her children the tender, grim wisdom of her struggle with the world. An executive wearing tailored underwear and flowing silk gowns. A woman president who makes difficult decisions when she has her period, because that is precisely when she is most emotional and most open therefore to the wisdom of strong feeling. A woman of the world who yet retains a quality of exuberance and joy that comes from the assertion of natural power and is far more compelling than innocence. A woman rugged on the outside who is also blatantly warm and sensitive and humorous and engaged and who is therefore far more potent in these qualities than a ''beguiling'' woman has ever been known to be.

Imitating the transformative rite our generation so urgently needs, this reshaping and re-dressing of the female body threatens to make us (in spite of our sexy new lingerie) into nothing more than a sorry form of pseudo-man—as if we had been caught perpetually in the stage of cross-gender experimentation and could not make our way through to the next essential purpose of the rite. For it is clear, of course, that in the tribal setting women take off the male clothes they have used for purposes of experimental androgynization and then move on into the ultimate goal of female initiation—the teaching of the inherent value of woman's life and work.

IV

As MEMBERS OF A culture that has consistently despised and denigrated women's activities, it cannot be easy for us to rediscover their meaning. And so we cast off all that we have known of our inherited, traditional values because the struggle for an evolved social identity would be that much easier if we simply became men. We give up our bodies, our appetites, our hunger for the authentic evolution and discovery of our selves; we cast off our emotions and intuitions, sacrificing the tender fierceness of our capacity to nourish and love. Willingly, we make ourselves less than all we might be for the dazzling right to participate at last in culture. And then, inexplicably, we find ourselves unable to move, caught in an obsession that gradually, day by day, draws us from all other enterprises into its sterile and repetitive heart.

We have noticed before now that an obsession has two faces. On the one hand it keeps us turning endlessly in a cycle of tedious preoccupation that confines and limits our development. But on the other hand, viewed symbolically, it expands, it deepens, it opens out and points vigorously to missing dimensions of our lives. What, then, might we say about an obsession with food that could show how it is an effort to achieve the most essential purpose of a female rite of passage? For in the tribal hut, where the relatives and older women gather to instruct the girls, the basic teaching transmits knowledge of the inherent sacrality of female life. "The education given is general," Eliade writes: "it consists in the revelation of the sacrality of women. The girl is ritually prepared to assume her specific mode of being, that is, to become a creatress, and at the same time is taught her responsibilities in society and in the cosmos, responsibilities which . . . are always religious in nature."

It is difficult for us to appreciate the radical nature of these words. This emphasis upon the creative nature of the female seems at first hearing to assign us to the service of the cradle and the diaper pail and to entrap us, all over again, in the most conservative notions of biology as destiny that have restricted our development all along.

Indeed, it is precisely this movement into woman's consecrated role that takes place in the tribal initiation rite. There, women are separated from the mother so that they may leave childhood and enter tribal life as those who will shortly become mothers themselves. Clearly then, the rite of passage as it was practiced in tribal culture cannot serve us as an exact model. We have not come this far to start it up all over again, stripping ourselves of our newly acquired "male" attributes, as Mariel Hemingway stripped off her new, muscular body to end up as she did, the luscious "tomato" of the 1980s, all decked out in seductiveness before we are served up to the family's hunger.

Yet, this notion of the inherent sacredness of women's lives may be taken in the broadest possible sense so that it can serve to remind us how for the last five thousand years, at least, we have practiced arts of creation, nurturance, and healing, sacred arts which, in their domestic form, have been disparaged, torn from their basic sacred meaning, and offered back to us both as lesser activities and as justification for limiting our social development. It is precisely at this juncture, where we have lost an essential understanding of ourselves, that food serves both to bring us back into an older stratum of associations and simultaneously to suggest the way we might elaborate new meanings.

And so we take up once again this task of reexamining the commonplace, of stripping away the overlay of conventional associations with which the lives of women are burdened. For food, after all, has defined female identity not only through the domestic routine of daily means—that endless, tedious round of supermarket, refrigerator, table, and kitchen sink from which we are so legitimately eager to free ourselves. It has defined more even than the history of mother/daughter relations and that early sorrow and disorder that began, for many of us, at the mother's breast. Dating back to our earliest impressions of life, recorded in the symbolic code of food imagery, the vanished story of female value and power returns to us again and again in our obsession with food—if only we learn to understand its meaning.

At the heart of an eating obsession is a regression to the infantile condition, not solely for the purpose of rebirth or in the hope of uncovering the buried history of our earliest bonds. Hidden behind our obsessive preoccupation with food is a need to regain a relationship to the sacral mystery of female being—a mystery conferred inalienably upon women's lives by our ability to create life and food from the female body, to sustain life through it, to succor and soothe through it our oldest terrors. It is as if we are trying to remind ourselves, through our obsessive overevaluation of food, that we have been starved of this positive sense of an inherent female creative power on the basis of which we could elaborate a new and meaningful female social identity.

It is fascinating, in this regard, to consider how deeply this first experience of food and eating at a woman's breast has influenced our notions of the sacred. William James, in his classic study of religious experience, observed the tendency to use metaphors of food and eating and drinking to describe the often ineffable sense of relationship to the divine.

> *Religious language clothes itself in such poor symbols as our life affords, and the whole organism gives overtones of comment whenever the mind is strongly stirred to expression. Language drawn from eating and drinking is probably as common in religious literature as is language drawn from the sexual life. We "hunger and thirst" after righteousness; we "find the Lord a sweet savor"; we "taste and see that it is good." "Spiritual milk for American babes, drawn from the breasts of both testaments," is a sub-title of the once famous New England Primer, and Christian devotional literature indeed quite floats in milk, thought of from the point of view, not of the mother, but of the greedy babe.*
>
> *Saint Francois de Sales, for instance, thus describes the "orison of quietude": "In this state the soul is like a little child still at the breast, whose mother, to caress him whilst he is still in her arms, makes her milk distill into his mouth without his even moving his lips. So it is here . . . Our Lord desires that our will should be satisfied with sucking the milk which His Majesty pours into our mouth, and that we should relish the sweetness without even knowing that it cometh from the Lord." And again: "Consider the little infants, united and joined to the breasts of their nursing mothers, you will see that from time to time they press themselves closer by little starts to which the pleasure of sucking prompts them. Even so, during its orison, the heart united to its God oftentimes makes attempts at closer union by movements during which it presses closer upon the divine sweetness."*

This imagery is, of course, particularly striking within a patriarchal religious tradition, where our only sanctioned view clothes the divine in masculine form. Apparently, however, the actual content of religious consciousness tells a different story and provides God the Father with attributes of the human mother, reminding us how potently our memories of the breast continue to influence all later experiences of moral and religious life. Indeed, if we followed the implications of this spontaneous food imagery far enough, we might well end by postulating the existence of God the Mother and so achieve an image of the divine that would restore to women their rightful place in the tradition of sacred power. Whatever this radical reversal did ultimately to our view of the world and the powers that rule it, certainly it would give to women in crisis about their identity a powerful incentive to proceed in pride and dignity as female beings, with our full mythic and sacral power restored to us.

Thus we arrive once again at that first experience of eating. Led back through the manifold associations we make to food, we are permitted yet again to derive from it essential lessons about the true nature of female being—lessons that would then allow us to elaborate an image of female identity that need not dress itself up in masculine traits.

Elizabeth Cady Stanton, at seventy-two years of age, understood this problem. "We who like the children of Israel," she said to the International Council of Women in 1888, "have been wandering in the wilderness of prejudice and ridicule for forty years feel a peculiar tenderness for the young women on whose shoulders we are about to leave our burdens. . . . The younger women are starting with great advantages over us. They have the results of our experience; they have superior opportunities for education; they will find a more enlightened public sentiment for discussion; they will have more courage to take the rights which belong to them. . . . Thus far women have been the mere echoes of men. Our laws and constitutions, our creeds and codes, and the customs of social life are all of masculine origin. The true woman is as yet a dream of the future.''

Whatever Elizabeth herself may have meant by this dream of the future, she is speaking to us, the legitimate inheritors of that earlier generation's burden—warning us, almost a hundred years before our time, that our struggle for the true woman must not take place in an imitation of masculine social forms. It is precisely, indeed, because we have not heard this warning that our movement forward, into ourselves, is now paralyzed in our obsession with food.

For food, in fact, preserves the silenced history of women's power. From infancy and through all the stages of our later development, women have exhibited in their relation to food capacities and qualities they have surrendered in many other aspects of their lives. Adept at the mysteries of creating bread from a cup of water, a handful of flour, a pinch of salt, a woman serves up the loaf that is the bread of life—exhibiting in the bowls and retorts of her domestic alchemy the awesome power of transforming matter into nurturance. Skilled in the preparation of those healing infusions of chamomile tea to relieve a belly ache, soft gelatin for a flu, cranberries without sugar to help with nausea, she all along was the mother-magician, adept at the healing arts. This woman, the mother, is the bringer of tradition through food into daily life. Ordering the buying of food and the serving of meals, she has ordered all those occasions of family cohesion, our return to one another from the divisiveness and harshness of our separate lives. And so, through food, she has expressed that very world of female value we are tempted to cast aside—its concern for nuance and subtlety. She knows the favorite dish for every member of her large family. We come, broken-hearted, home from college and a failed love affair, exhausted by a day's labor in the study or the legal chamber. She remembers that honey cake that comforted us as a child, knocks at the door to our room, offers us a tray of her compassion.

Daily, year after year, from earliest infancy, we have received from our mothers, in the way they offered and ordered food, an eloquent expression of the values by which women have lived: life ordered, three times daily, serenely composed, the napkin under the fork to the left of the plate, small glass three-quarters filled with juice, the basket set out with fruit for adornment.

Is it the need for these qualities of female life that draws us to food? Draws us, ropes us in, fixes us in a repetitive cycle of longing and renunciation, desire and purge of desire—in this time especially, when we are so tempted to disparage women's values and distinctive modes of being.

Our ambivalence, our conflict, our uncertainty, our movements forward and our retreats are nowhere so apparent as in our ambiguous relationship to food, with its peerless associative capacities, its powerful resonances and conjuring abilities.

Proust the dreamer dips a piece of Madeleine in a cup of tea and conjures up the vanished world of his Combray childhood. Lawrence Durrell puts an olive in his mouth and experiences through it "the whole Mediterranean—the sculptures, the palms, the gold beads, the bearded heroes, the wine, the ideas, the ships, the moonlight, the winged gorgons, the bronze men, the philosophers—all of it," he says, "seems to rise in the sour, pungent taste of these black olives between the teeth." And we, women of this modern age, in danger of thrusting aside our most awesome and mysterious heritage, susceptible too to this conjuring power of food, taste and evoke for ourselves the hidden sacral truths of our fundamental being as women, as they have come down to us in our mothers' milk and in all subsequent food offerings from the first moments of our existence.

In an eating disorder, food comes to provide the diverse, apparently contradictory functions that form the rite of passage. It helps the young woman to separate from her mother through the foods she eats and purchases and prepares. But it also serves to bond the woman to her mother through a shared preoccupation. At the same time, it connects her to traditional female values at a time of immense social upheaval and change. And, finally, it introduces her to the lost, sacred dimension of women's lives. In this sense, our relationship to food has all the significant features of a tribal rite of passage. No wonder then we are so addicted to our preoccupations with it. If women today were encouraged to evolve authentic rituals for themselves, in which they could move knowingly through the transitional passage required by every woman who enters culture, we would not have to purge our appetites and plunder our bodies as a means to express our need for transformation.

Then we might be able to exploit the power of our preoccupation with food to lead us into all the slumbering powers of female being we presently disparage. For surely in these lives of ours there is some way to become the mother without taking on her sacrifice? Surely we can order and heal and care for and nourish without simultaneously giving up all else we might become? Surely there is a way to set food down upon the table without ourselves becoming the meal that is served.

There is something within us—and it is loyal, devoted, and striving, moreover, for wholeness and completion—that will not allow us simply to turn and cast away these mother-lives that haunt us at this moment of developmental urgency and transformation, when we are so eager to leave our mother behind and enter this culture that has always excluded us. Our mothers may not be able to model for us the new women we need to become, but there is in their lives much of value we need to take with us over that great divide that separates us from culture.

Indeed, we have little choice in this matter. For if we are unable to recover the sacred dimension of women's traditional life as we enter culture, we shall be driven to hold it unknowingly, clutching a handful of prized recipes, secrets of the kitchen, that cut in the loaf that lets the bread rise without bursting, the special ingredient in the holiday honey cake, these foods we seek sometimes all over the world, yearning through our attachment to them for that childhood sense of the mother in her fierce mystery and tender power—giver, upholder, and preserver of life.

This transfiguration of value, in the name of our mothers and ourselves, is hot and radical work. And in it, I propose, is our eventual liberation from obsession. When we can stop in our great rush forward long enough to appreciate the qualities of female life for which food stands, we will not require this obsessive concern with eating as a reminder of all that we are in danger of casting from us, prematurely.

These valiant, disparaged mothers of ours—is it possible we shall finally be able to separate from them only when we discover simultaneously how to leave behind the traditional roles by which they have been entrapped and how to reinvest the traditional values by which they have lived with their oldest mythic sense of meaning? That is the type of ritual practice we need, filled with careful distinctions and with forgiveness—both of ourselves and of our mothers. And for this an obsession, with all its hidden rage and disguised conflict, cannot serve us.

This is subtle work in which we are engaged. It requires weighing and measuring, the search for the right combinations of ingredients (traditional female qualities measured against what have been regarded as exclusive masculine rights). It requires ceaseless experimentation, a pinch of this, a handful of that. It cannot be learned from any cookbook of recipes presently available to us, but it can draw on the traditional ways women have always worked, kneading and pounding and substituting and adapting and inventing, all along converting the kitchen into that ceremonial ground of transformations.

But above all, this effort to evolve the new woman asks a fierce, pigheaded faith in the knowledge that women have a right to the type of transformational passage the obsession with food attempts so bitterly, so tragically, and so persistently to provide. Imagine a generation of women bringing to the work of self-evolution the same devotion, the same discipline, the same dedication, the same militant care and concern for detail they presently invest in their search for the perfect diet to bring about that ideal body of transformation our generation seeks. Imagine this struggle freed from the futile symbolism of obsession and converted into the expressive symbolism of ritual. Imagine us, sleeves rolled up for the task, aprons donned, rolling pins brandished, as we straighten up these shoulders of ours on which the first generation of our foremothers in struggle placed their burdens. Imagine us shaping that new woman, dream of the future, out of the transformed obsessions that presently rule our lives.

Notes

Part One: Identity

Page 13 A suggestive discussion of the difference in eating patterns between men and women appeared in the *Radcliffe News,* April 1983. The article reports the findings of a preliminary study of Radcliffe and Harvard students conducted during the spring of 1982. "Preliminary findings show striking differences between men and women in eating patterns and feelings about weight and body size. Women are more likely than men to be either dissatisfied with their weight or to feel that they should be thinner. More than 80 percent of the women reported that they would like to lose weight, while fewer than half of the men felt this way. Only about a third of the men said that they had ever been on a diet to lose weight, while more than three-quarters of the women had been on a diet at some point. Women also reported much more frequent dieting than did men, with about a third of the women reporting that they diet almost all of the time."

Page 13 The discussion of college women suffering from eating disorders can be found in the October 1983 issue of *Ms.*

Page 16 Betty Friedan, *The Feminine Mystique* (New York: Dell, 1974).

Page 20 One hundred forty-four laxatives a day is neither an approximation nor an exaggeration. This number was reported by the *San Francisco Sunday Examiner and Chronicle*, October 31, 1982.

Page 22 Debbie's story was described in the October 31 article cited above.

Page 22 Erikson's discussion of identity crisis as a turning point in development can be found in his *Identity, Youth and Crisis* (New York and London: Norton, 1968).

Page 23 "More middle-aged women are admitting that they starve themselves in order to be thin," Nadine Brozan writes. The survey is reported by Brozan in the *New York Times*.

Page 28 Articles by young feminists appeared in *Ms.*, April 1983.

Page 30 I received numerous unsolicited letters, poems, and personal accounts in response to my book *The Obsession: Reflections on the Tyranny of Slenderness* (New York: Harper & Row, 1981). This particular excerpt is from a short story by Kimberly Kluger-Bell entitled "The Hunger." Through an unfortunate error, this credit was omitted in first edition of *The Hungry Self.*

Page 32 These particular references to Susan B. Anthony and Elizabeth Cady Stanton appeared in an article on women's courage by Louise Bernikow in *Mademoiselle*, May 1982.

Page 34 My thumbing through popular magazines and newspapers has turned up far more articles on what is now being called the "Mannish Look" than I could possibly include in my discussion. Both pictures and verbal descriptions of the new styles leave no doubt whatever that women are dressing in men's clothes. For instance, from the *New York Times Magazine*, June 24, 1984: "The men's-wear influence is seen almost everywhere in the new fall clothes." From *Vanity Fair*, July

Notes

1984: "In Paris they call them 'Les Garconnes'—girls with a penchant for dressing up in boyish attire. Their hair Eton-cropped, their legs trouser-clad, they stride along the boulevards." And, from the *New York Times,* May 4, 1984: "The Mannish Look Takes Over." Needless to say, these mannish styles call for a woman to be lean and slender, slim-hipped, flat-chested. When, however, the female body takes on bulk and approaches male looks from this heftier side of things, society is far less welcoming. The *Los Angeles Times,* September 26, 1982, published an article about a young woman who was told that she would have to lose weight if she wanted to march as a drum majorette. "Drum Majorette Told She Can't Look Like Line-backer," says the headline.

Part Two: Mothers and Daughters

Page 42 There is a fascinating discussion of the way in which the mother's frustrations are transmitted to the daughter through food in Angelyn Spignesi's essential book, *Starving Women: A Psychology of Anorexia* (Dallas: Spring, 1983). Dr. Spignesi shows how the mother restrains the daughter and simultaneously pushes her into more creative realms while remembering her own failed attempts. The book also includes a comprehensive review of the literature on the mother/daughter bond in eating disorders.

Page 47 My book about my mother's life and family is *In My Mother's House* (New York: Ticknor & Fields, 1983). It is also available in paperback (New York: Harper & Row, 1984).

Page 51 The quotation from Frederick V. Grunfeld can be found in *Prophets Without Honor: A Background to Freud, Kafka, Einstein and Their World* (New York: McGraw-Hill, 1980), p. 28.

Page 55 Russell Baker's autobiography, *Growing Up,* was published by New American Library in 1982.

Page 57 A study of a male anorexic appears in Steven Levenkron's book, *Treating and Overcoming Anorexia Nervosa* (New York: Charles Scribner's Sons, 1982). Levenkron notes that "a male anorexic is atypical," but does not explore the reasons for this atypicality.

Page 61 Aimee Liu, *Solitaire* (New York: Harper & Row, 1979), p. 128.

Page 79 Quotation from Thomas Carlyle can be found in *I Too Am Here,* edited by Alan and May Simpson (Cambridge: Cambridge University Press, 1977). For a superb general discussion of attitudes toward women at the turn of the century, see *The Ideas of the Woman's Suffrage Movement, 1890–1920,* by Arlene S. Kraditor (New York: Doubleday/Anchor, 1971).

Page 86 I am grateful to Joyce Lindenbaum for numerous discussions on the problem of envy between women.

Page 88 A description of the mothers of anorectic women, which supports my observations, can be found in Hilda Bruch's important book, *The Golden Cage: The Enigma of Anorexia Nervosa* (New York: Vintage, 1979).

Page 90 About the atmosphere of mystification in which daughters are raised: "In spite of the fact that I was encouraged to excel," says a woman in her late thirties who is struggling to become a writer, "there was an unwritten rule: 'Don't be better than me.' And anytime I tried to be I was slapped down." This is a particularly insightful comment; I have, however, heard similar comments from most women who have begun to reflect on their childhoods.

Notes

Page 93 For a further discussion of the way in which the daughter turns her anger at her mother against her own body, see my book *The Obsession: Reflections on the Tyranny of Slenderness* (New York: Harper & Row, 1982).

Part Three: The Primal Feast

Page 97 Initial quotation from M.F.K. Fisher, *The Art of Eating* (New York: Vintage, 1976), p. 353.

Page 98 Elias Canetti, *Crowds and Power* (New York: Continuum, 1971), quoted by Sheila Macleod, *The Art of Starvation* (New York: Schocken, 1982).

Page 99 The quotations from Erikson may be found in his *Childhood and Society* (New York: Norton, 1950).

Page 102 The story about the actress and her daughter appears in Fisher's *Art of Eating*, p. 359.

Page 117 The description of the work of Melanie Klein is by Cecil Mushatt, M.D., M.Sc., from *Envy and Gratitude and Other Works, 1946–1963* (New York: Delacorte Press, 1975).

Page 117 Melanie Klein, *The Psychoanalysis of Children*, revised ed. (New York: Dell, 1975).

Page 119 Melanie Klein, *Love, Guilt and Reparation and Other Works* (New York: Delacorte Press, 1975).

Page 122 The discussion of telepathic communication between mother and infant is from Thomas Ogden, *Projective Identification and Psychotherapeutic Technique* (New York: Jason Aronson, 1982). Ogden is quoting R. Spitz, *The First Year of Life*.

Page 128 The relationship between male aggression and male feelings of vulnerability is discussed by Susan Griffin in *Pornography and Silence* (New York: Harper & Row, 1980).

Page 135 Reay Tannahill, *Flesh and Blood: A History of the Cannibal Complex* (London: Hamish Hamilton, 1975).

Page 136 Angelyn Spignesi, in *Starving Women*, discusses the anorexic's sacrifice of blood in terms of serving the rage and hungers of an archetypal mother. For a study of infantile experience of the mother, the reader is referred to the work of D. W. Winnicott, Michael Balint, Margaret Mahler, and Dorothy Dinnerstein.

Page 144 Golda Meir, *My Life* (New York: Dell, 1975), p. 12.

Page 154 Marcel Proust, *Swann's Way,* translated by C. K. Scott Moncrieff (New York: Heritage Press, 1922), pp. 46, 48.

Page 157 The sources of the various quotes, in order, are: "Blue water and yellow ships," from Ellen Glasgow, *The Sheltered Life* (New York: Hill and Wang, 1979), p. 10; "We would come in from school," from Chernin, *In My Mother's House*; "Then my dear mamma," from Fisher, *The Art of Eating,* p. 86.

Part Four: Rites of Passage

Pages 165–66 References to Mircea Eliade are from *Rites and Symbols of Initiation* (New York: Harper Torchbooks, 1958).

Page 167 In a discussion of the significance of food in *Starving Women,* Angelyn Spignesi shows the affliction to be a ritual entry into psychic and sacred realms. She also sees the tragic problem in the syndrome: "The suffering of every starving woman is that the opening to the wealth of psyche and the tyrannical defense against that opening are in her experience at the same time.''

Page 178 The *Ms.* article on eating disorders among college women can be found in the October 1983 issue.

Page 180 The quote from Renee, the senior at the University of Arizona, is from *Ms.,* October 1983, p. 420.

Pages 180–81 Andrew Weil, *The Marriage of the Sun and the Moon: A Quest for Unity in Consciousness* (Boston: Houghton Mifflin, 1980).

Page 182 Fisher, *The Art of Eating,* pp. 382–84.

Page 189 The story about Mariel Hemingway is from *People,* November 21, 1983.

Pages 197–98 The quotations from William James are from *The Variety of Religious Experience* (New York: Modern Library, 1902), pp. 12–13.

Pages 199–200 The quotation from Elizabeth Cady Stanton is from *Feminism: The Essential Historical Writings,* edited by Miriam Schneir (New York: Vintage, 1972).

Page 201 Lawrence Durrell, *Prospero's Cell* (London: Penguin Books, 1960), p. 96.

Acknowledgments

I<small>T IS A SOURCE</small> of great joy that my friends have been woven into the pages of this work, which would not have taken its present form without them.

To Angelyn Spignesi I am deeply grateful for *Starving Women: A Psychology of Anorexia* and for compelling conversations on the themes of eating disorders as interrupted ritual and the mother/daughter mythological patterns in anorexia. She was also a sensitive reader of the manuscript, even where she disagreed with my formulations.

Michael Rogin and I have discussed Melanie Klein and the oral dramas of infantile life for many years, along with most of the other issues raised in this book. He read every draft of this manuscript, provided invaluable criticism, and gave me exactly the right editorial advice at precisely the moment it was needed.

Louise Bernikow read the first draft of the manuscript and offered extremely helpful commentary and critique.

Diane Cleaver, my agent, has supported my work in every possible way. I am grateful for her sound advice and for her outstanding critical acumen.

My editor, Elisabeth Scharlatt, has once again made her presence felt on every page. She is the kind of editor every writer hopes to find someday. Devoted both to the smallest details and to the largest strategies of presentation, she has given me essential help throughout.

Rebecca Busselle introduced me to the work of M.F.K. Fisher and shared with me her own joyful knowledge of fine eating and good food. I am grateful to her both for our discussions about this book and for the way she and Sam and Katrina and Max made me feel at home on the East Coast during its composition.

Marsha Angus, Karin Carrington, Cathy Galligher, Roz Parenti, and Lillian Rubin have all been part of countless conversations that have found their way into these pages in unchartable ways. For this, and for their friendship, I shall always be grateful.

Florence Spignesi made me feel warm and welcome during my first New England winter. I am happy to have this opportunity to thank her.

Finally, to the women whose lives and stories appear in these pages I am deeply indebted. Their struggle and courage has heartened and inspired me.